ITI CONFERENCE 3

Proceedings

ITI CONFERENCE 3

Proceedings

Edited by
Catriona Picken

Proceedings of the third annual conference of the
Institute of Translation and Interpreting

28–29 April 1989
Hotel Russell, London

First published in 1989
by Aslib, The Association for Information Management
Information House
20–24 Old Street
London EC1V 9AP

British Library Cataloguing in Publication Data

Institute of Translation and Interpreting, *Conference. (3rd
: 1989 : London, England)*.
ITI Conference 3 : proceedings of the third annual
conference of the Institute of Translation and
Interpreting, 28–29 April 1989, Hotel Russell, London.
1. Languages.   Translation
I. Title   II. Picken, Catriona, *1934–*
418'.02

ISBN 0–85142–256–X

Printed and bound in Great Britain by
Henry Ling, Ltd. at the Dorset Press,
Dorchester, Dorset

Contents

Conference Committee

Roger Fletcher (Chairman)
Dr Marie-Josée Andreasen
David Beattie
Hugh Keith
Pamela Mayorcas
Mike Shields
Albin Tybulewicz
Hilde Watson
Dimity Castellano (Secretary)

Introduction

Catriona Picken

For this, the third annual conference of the Institute of Translation and Interpreting, there was no announced theme, no keynote speaker. Both of these decisions were keenly debated both by the conference committee and the ITI council, and certainly the number of people coming to the conference was comparable with the previous year, and attendance at the sessions was consistently high, so that indicates that they were not put off! A theme means that, by and large, the papers presented have a link, however tenuous, with that theme. Were the topics at ITI 3 too disparate? I think probably not, and as the conference progressed, a theme emerged anyway – training.

Our President, Professor Juan Sager, foreshadowed what was to come in his opening remarks, when he said, 'What we have to work out for ourselves is how we should organise our profession, in order to maintain the highest standards'.

Readers of these *Proceedings* will soon become aware of this underlying theme, whether they start at Session 1 and read straight through to Tony Hartley's summary, or whether they go first for the topic they find most interesting, and then read the other papers later. To start the conference, Doug Embleton and John Graham, both from the (big) business world, laid emphasis on training. Doug is not only a translator, but also provides language training for his non-linguist fellow-employees at ICI. John gives an account of the extremely thorough translator training process at Mannesmann. John Murphy told us how, if we have not already done so, we shall all have to train ourselves to deal with electronic document transfer in the near future, and in similar vein Sue Halbert described the very real benefits such systems can bring to those who work from home, as is the case with many freelances. Sue was describing a long-established group of telecommuters. 'The work-pattern of the future' was her sub-title, and many staff translators as well as freelances were interested in these possibilities.

Session 3 actually had the title *Training*, with Hugh Keith discussing the rival merits of university and in-service training and Karin Band making us all aware of the vital need for continuing education ('top-up' and 'keep-up' subsequently became the key-words for the whole conference). Session 4 on legal and ethical issues was in a way a lesson for us all, focusing as it did on the maintenance of professional standards and the legal consequences if anything goes wrong. It was unfortunately not possible to obtain any record of the informal presentations made by the panel speakers, but the discussion which followed is fully reported. Session 5, although entitled *Translation forum*, also touched on the training theme in its first paper, with Ben Teague describing how he tackles new areas of knowledge for translation purposes. Mike Hollow's fascinating account of what goes on at BBC Monitoring, with particular emphasis on Soviet broadcasting, made me for one feel profoundly grateful that there are such brilliant and dedicated people to convey all the foreign news to us.

The interpreters were well served at their very own session, with Lucy Collard giving a down-to-earth account of the realities of training the trainers of community interpreters and Michael Francis giving us an insight into the way an interpreter's mind *has* to work.

To judge from Geoffrey Kingscott's survey of the literature of translation, which opened the last session, the worst way to learn anything about translation or interpreting as a profession is to read novels or see plays with translators or interpreters as principal characters! But Geoff also covered the rest of the ground so thoroughly that I am sure we shall all be adding several titles to our reading list. The Professional Associations' presentations (not available in written form) were followed by the usual lively discussion which took up the topics introduced by the panel, with strong emphasis on what is known as 'user-eduacation' – in other words, how can we put ourselves across?

In his final *Summary*, Tony Hartley not only looked back over the conference, but took the opportunity to suggest 'items on the agenda of future meetings of the ITI'. This constructive approach is always welcome. If readers of these *Proceedings* feel that there are any topics which need more detailed treatment or have not yet been discussed at all, please contact the ITI* with your views.

The continuing success of the ITI conferences depends to a great extent on feedback from you, the readers.

As always, I am happy to have the opportunity to express my appreciation to all those who helped with organising the conference and to offer a sincere thank you to the rapporteurs, whose contribution to the *Proceedings* is indispensable.

*Institute of Translation and Interpreting, 318a Finchley Road, London NW3 5HT.

Opening remarks

Juan Sager

President, ITI

Welcome to the Third International Conference of the Institute of Translation and Interpreting. This annual event now seems to be a regular meeting point for the profession and a testimony to the growing strength of the Institute.

We are meeting as a family to talk about our concerns and it is right that we should do this when all around us there are so many exhortations about 1992, accompanied by so much confusion about what should be done to drag this country out of its monoglot stupor. None of this is news to our profession as we continue providing the services that have always been and will always be in demand.

The confidence of the Institute in staging an important annual forum for issues concerned with interpreting and translation is shown by two departures from last year's pattern. There is no special theme and there is no keynote speaker.

If a theme had to be chosen, it clearly would have had to be 'consolidation in strength' or simply 'business as usual', and this can be seen from the programme and the list of topics before us. Not having a theme also saves us from having our theme copied by others; or should we take comfort from the fact that our theme of last year, which was 'languages mean business' was borrowed by the CBI/CILT conference of January last with a slight modification? It called itself *Languages means business*, probably borrowing the idea for the 's' in *means* from the 'meanz' used in advertising a popular product in a range of 57 varieties. Or, should we say that what the Institute of Translation and Interpreting does today, others do tomorrow?

A keynote speaker could either tell us how great the demand is for our services, something we know already, or alternatively tell the rest of the world what services we can provide. What they cannot tell us and what we have to work out for ourselves, is how we should organise our profession, in order to maintain the highest standards, to train newcomers and to make our clients understand that we cannot work miracles of international sympathy and understanding. They do *not*, but we *do* know that interpreters and translators are not made overnight, that there is a limited pool of talent available and that the much talked about need for people to acquire a second language is not going to happen for a number of reasons. The simple fact is, that despite loud protestations from ministers of education about a national curriculum which will make every pupil study a language to at least O level, language learning in schools has been in continuous decline. The provision of language graduates with Postgraduate Certificates of Education has declined by 25 per cent (from 911 to 687) over the last 10 years; and the number of pupils taking A levels in French, the bastion of language provision in schools, has dropped by 14 per cent over the last 20 years (from an already low 25,600 to 22,100). On this basis the country will have to import linguists to meet the challenge of 1992. Our task is to focus on training for our profession and there is a full session devoted to this subject.

The other topic which we could have chosen as a theme is the so-called 'language industry', the latest buzz-word around which a number of large conferences are currently being organised. This topic would appear to be relevant to our profession but what does it mean to us? 'Language industry' is, in the first instance, a loan translation from the French *les industries de la langue*. But like so many slogans it combines the deceptive ease of internationalism with semantic vacuity. So we have to interpret the possible meaning of the juxtaposition of these two nouns. Is the language industry an industry 'for' or 'of' language? What are the raw materials of this industry, what are the products or services it provides?

On the one hand there has always been a support industry for communication of all sorts from which interpreting and translating have benefited. We could therefore associate the beginning of the language industry with the start-up of industrial printing. The telephone, the wireless, the dictaphone, the typewriter and telex and, more recently, fax, word-processors and electronic mail are all tools that we have used to overcome the barriers of time and distance in communication. They are now part of our everyday lives and appropriately they are discussed at our conferences as a regular item. But they are only tools for human use and do not directly help to overcome the biggest barrier of all, that of a second language, which is the *raison d'être* of our profession.

If we interpret language industry as processes that manipulate or help us to manipulate language then we are in the field of computational linguistics if, like me, your background lies in language and linguistics, but in the field of natural language processing if you approach the problem from the point of view of the computer scientist. There is a strange division of approaches and terminology between these two orientations which might itself benefit from a good translation and interpreting service. (It is strange world in which 'speech analysis', for example, is not considered part of 'natural language processing', and 'dialogue' is restricted to interaction with machines.) If you follow fashion you will, of course, also want to know that NLP is considered part of Information Technology, another suitably vague expression which may compete with Language Industry for the collective name that describes the various software tools now available to assist us in our work.

There is no doubt that we have benefited from the tools in the form of dictionaries and lexical databases that are now available in a wide range of formats and modes of access. The CD-ROM dictionary evolution is undoubtedly a major breakthrough which will lead to a range of reference tools that we have always dreamt of but never thought possible. These tools are now industrially viable but price and usefulness of content are not yet in balance to encourage many professionals to invest in them.

The other part of the industry which could directly affect us, namely, Machine Translation in its various forms from assistance to full independent translation, is going through a period of welcome introspection and this conference does not specifically address it. The feasibility of the computer performing transfer operations between languages has been proved, the openness of the market for such tools has been tested and in the process the requirements of consumers have been more realistically defined. It is now time for the industry to produce its prototypes or to move from prototypes where they exist to full product development.

A third interpretation of language industry is an industry which produces language in the form of automatic abstracts and, of course, also fully automatic translation without human intervention, or even languages in the form of indexing and documentation languages or the so called 'natural language interfaces' or 'front-ends' to a variety of computer systems. This form of industry might be seen as a competitor with the profession, but we know that this is not the case. On the contrary, here we are in the realm of restricted languages for highly specialised communication. The implications of these developments for interpreting and translating are most exciting, but work in this area is so far research only and quite a distance away from industrial development. This may be a topic for a future conference.

Finally, I note with interest the range of professional background and geographical provenance of our speakers. They show once more that interpreting and translating have no natural boundaries of any kind. As our skills are needed in any area of human contact, we have a foot in every branch of culture, industry and science, commerce and technology and can therefore immediately react to and benefit from innovation that facilitates our work.

Session 1: Business

Chaired by Beryl Rice

The role of the translator or translation department in the company

Doug Embleton

ICI Chemicals & Polymers Ltd, Wilton, Middlesbrough, Cleveland

On the day before I travelled to the Conference I was talking to a Japanese colleague at work. We were discussing a newspaper article about a well-known British retailer of clothing, household fabrics and furnishings which, in its initial marketing exercise in Japan, had not done its homework. Japanese homes tend to be smaller than ours and, in consequence, so does the furniture.

Our conversation then embraced the many areas which *should* overlap and interact in order to make an organisation truly international. My Japanese colleague proceeded to draw some diagrams to show his perception of a fundamental difference between Japanese and British organisations. To illustrate the Japanese organisation he drew a series of slightly overlapping circles and explained that while each department or function within the organisation exercised its own perceived, specialist role there had to be an overlap – in terms of dialogue or contact – to enable the organisation to function as a whole. His diagrammatic view of some British organisations was a series of totally separate circles. My experience of talking to and with gatherings of industrialists, educationalists, language trainers, translators and interpreters has given me the impression that the separate circles are moving closer together but that there is still some way to go before they overlap.

On reading the Proceedings of last year's ITI Conference I was interested, but far from daunted, to read that only six people had agreed with the concept of the 'overall linguist'. I subsequently contacted these six people and we have decided to form a breakaway group of the ITI, to be named the Institute of Overall Linguists.

On closer examination, it transpired that the term 'overall linguist' had been applied to the personal combination of translating and interpreting skills. I would like to widen this debate and examine the concept of the 'language co-ordinator' as a potential role in industry and commerce. In fact, the title of my presentation could be readily revised to 'the role of the *language service* in the company'. It could well be that I represent the alternative definition of an 'overall linguist'. If the quick repair to the Swiss-manufactured compressor on one of our chemical plants means less lost production and sales, and if the Swiss engineers do not speak English, I am happy literally to don the 'overalls'.

I am equally happy to arrange EFL tuition for an incoming secondee from Japan – and for his family. The next item on the day's agenda may be a request from a publicity manager to co-ordinate the translation and proofreading of some technical literature for an exhibition. This could be followed by the need to contact a freelance translator or to prepare multilingual Transport Emergency Cards for the road transport of a chemical product.

Longer term objectives may include a language needs survey of another location within the organisation or a review of the foreign language requirements of, for example, a construction project or foreign acquisition. The co-ordination of these and many other tasks from within the organisation demands access to and the use of a whole range of external resources and suppliers – freelance translators, translation agencies, interpreters, teachers.

I would like to describe:

- the gradually increasing awareness within British industry of the need for language skills and services
- how such a co-ordinating role can be performed and marketed within the organisation
- examples of the ways in which the individual components of a language service interact and overlap
- the potential benefits of the 'language co-ordinator' role.

1992 AND ALL THAT

Attitudes in British industry have certainly changed since the publication in 1907 of a *Guide to British businessmen visiting Buenos Aires*. One of the first phrases in the book enables our visiting businessman to ask of his aspiring business partner, 'Can you prove to us that you are to be trusted?' Much more recently, a colleague of mine was on a business trip to a small town in West Germany. He needed to take a taxi to reach his appointment on time and rapidly gave his instructions in English. He then proceeded to pass the time of day quite happily with the driver who, at the end of the journey, asked my colleague how many taxi drivers in London speak German. My colleague was able to admit to himself that this remark not only caught him off-guard but also made him feel guilty. Was the taxi driver expressing a view which was shared by my colleague's German business contacts? Much the same could now be said of certain sectors of British industry. There *is* a growing awareness of our insularity in terms of language skills.

Using a 24-hour clock as a measurement scale of language consciousness one might say that British industry is at last waking up at 07.00. If ever a spur to action were needed, then surely the imminence of 1992 and the Single Market has provided that spur. On the same measurement scale of the 24-hour clock one might also say that many of our competitors are situated at 16.00. For example, the Japanese firm wishing to sell in Germany will use German-speaking employees and high quality trade literature. British industry is gradually waking up to the fact that the most important language is the language of the customer, whether it be in written or spoken form. I think that it is true to say that there has never been a greater opportunity for the various sectors of the language service industry, if I may be permitted to use such a term.

1992, or perhaps more accurately 1993 and beyond, has created a new market, the market of '1992 conferences'. I have recently been able to speak to separate gatherings of educationalists, language trainers, industrialists and translators. Out of this fairly recent and indeed welcome experience three key factors have emerged:

1. These individual groupings of providers and users do not cross each others' demarcated boundaries and talk with one another nearly enough.
2. More and more industrialists have, in a sense, taken the taxi ride to which I referred and now clearly recognise the need for language services, and ultimately for a language strategy within their organisation, but are uncertain of exactly what they need, what is available and what constitutes a quality product at a reasonable market rate. Many of us still experience the gasps of amazement when the cost of a professional service – and I emphasise the word 'professional' – is quoted.
3. This recognition by industry of the need for language services has to take its place amongst the many other business strategy priorities imposed by the Single Market.

Indeed, businessmen are in danger of being overwhelmed and even 'switched off' by mailshots from every conceivable sector of the language service industry, all offering the panacea to their 1992 problems. 'Let us train your staff, let us translate your trade literature, let us conduct a language needs analysis. . . .' The list is endless. In the short term, it is unlikely that most UK industrial or commercial organisations will set up their own in-house translation or language training departments on a scale equal to those which already exist in many organisations in continental Western Europe. A more viable short-term alternative is offered by the 'language co-ordinator', a post which could at least ensure that quality services from external providers are obtained from the truly professional practitioners such as yourselves.

ICI CHEMICALS & POLYMERS LTD

The role of the Languages Unit of ICI Chemicals & Polymers Ltd is 'to meet the changing – and increasing – foreign language needs of the business'. Since the business is a truly international business and since the Languages Unit currently operates with a relatively small number of in-house staff the effective co-ordinating of a wide range of external resources and services is vital. In a real sense, these external providers are an integral part of the language service.

Translations

Translations into English are carried out in-house and also by a panel of freelance translators. Some of the in-house translations are carried out orally and this direct contact with customers not only constitutes an invaluable technical familiarisation process for the translator, it can also engender a dialogue which reveals other language needs. Further, it enables us to find out what is going on and constitutes one of the overlapping circles mentioned above.

A database contains the references of some 20,000 internally generated translations, and new translations are reported worldwide to other locations within the organisation.

A word processing system caters for the production of mutilingual Transport Emergency Cards – TremCards – which must accompany any trans-European consignment of chemical products.

Interpreting

Clear distinctions are made between informal or ad hoc interpreting assignments and those more formal occasions which require the services of fully qualified interpreters. In the latter instance, for example, in the event of a press conference or visiting trade delegation, as much care as possible would be devoted to providing the interpreters with background documents and word lists. Informal interpreting, carried out only by those in-house staff who are willing and interested, may involve the repair or maintenance of a machine by a foreign engineer, technical discussions with foreign colleagues, suppliers or customers – or the unexpected arrival of a foreign lorry or tanker driver.

Product literature

The term 'product literature' covers a wide range of documents or brochures which are printed in foreign languages. These include technical literature, sales promotion brochures, customer magazines and newsletters, data sheets and advertisements. The English texts are sent for translation to our National Selling Company in the country of the target language and may be translated either by the in-house translator or by freelance translators in that country. Before being returned to the UK, the translation is checked by a product expert within the National Selling Company. On its return to the Languages Unit it will once again be checked, this time by English mother-tongue experts who will be looking for what I can best describe as the 'mirror effect', that is the mis-translation caused by any weakness or ambiguity in the original English text. There then follow the various proofreading stages which we are currently attempting to eliminate by interfacing floppy disk production of the translated texts with the typesetting equipment of the printer.

As a constant reminder of the pitfalls of this area of our work I keep the usual collection of translation howlers. These include a notice from a Turkish hotel bedroom which advises guests as follows: 'If service required, give two strokes to the maid . . . and one for the varlet'. Menus are also a reliable source and a Russian menu extols the virtues of 'mixed vegetables' as 'boiled combinations' – which may be an apt description of my presentation!

Language training

Language training packages have been developed over a period of many years. The Languages Unit essentially plays a co-ordinating and developmental role and the training itself is provided either by freelance teachers or by local colleges. At Wilton, the training is provided in classrooms which are located within the Languages Unit. This helps very much to create an 'open door' atmosphere and provides us with a constant influx of colleagues who are themselves increasingly aware of the role of foreign languages not only in their own jobs but also in ours.

Weekly classes are provided in a range of languages and at different levels. Examinations are held annually on-site. Closed group classes are arranged for common interest groups. Recent examples are a commissioning project involving secondments to Japan; people involved with an acquisition in France; the Technical Service (literally 'after-sales' service) staff of a specific product; a package designed to assist the launch of a new product in France.

Individual tuition is available whenever necessary and on a very flexible basis. The individual may be unable to attend a regular class or may have more urgent, business-related objectives. This tuition is also provided to secondees and their families and may well be linked with external, intensive courses. Authentic, job-related material may sometimes be used in these courses.

EFL tuition meets the needs of an increasing number of incoming secondees (and their families) and seems likely to increase as the organisation becomes more international. This has been extended to include liaison with local schools who will be receiving as pupils the children of incoming secondees. External, intensive courses are offered by a small number of language schools with whom we have forged a close relationship over many years.

Support materials are the obvious items such as cassettes and videos but also encompass a library of cultural background/cultural briefing books.

Surveys of language training requirements and of overall language needs have been carried out at several major locations and have not only provided useful information on the perceptions of departments and individuals of their language requirements. They have also acted as an invaluable 'marketing tool' for the language service. Surveys are conducted by means of questionnaires and interviews but may also involve presentations describing the language service to individual departments, businesses or locations. This dialogue is the best marketing tool I know. In any large organisation it is amazing how many people will say: 'But I didn't even know of the existence of your service'. Separate circles again!

ADVANTAGES OF LANGUAGE USE

These are the perceived advantages of language skills as revealed by four recent language surveys:

- personal relationship: establishing a personal rapport with customers and colleagues

- understanding others' needs: this includes an awareness of other cultures and preferred business styles
- respect and credibility: Anglocentricity no longer rules OK!
- feeling 'comfortable': good business relationships are not achieved if one feels alienated or marginalised
- extra information: a typical quote from one survey was 'I find that more information can be obtained by allowing people to relax in *their* language'.

The surveys were based on questionnaires and covered a total of 400 individuals. We have now begun to check these findings, initially on a small scale, with our National Selling Companies in Germany and France and have received confirmation that many of our products are effectively a 'technical sell'. This implies that our ability to participate fully in technical discussions with customers, to respond quickly to technical queries and to provide high quality technical literature in the language of the customer are integral components of the overall sales package.

All of these facts may well be obvious to the language professions. However, it may be advantageous to achieve a shift from some of the rhetoric of the current abundance of '1992 conferences' towards some hard evidence derived from the end users of language services. A good example of the way in which the various disciplines within a language service can interact and overlap was offered by the acquisition of a production site in northern France some years ago. The language service effectively became a member of the project team and in doing so we were able to get to know some of our new French colleagues. The package of language services which was provided during the first year of the project covered most of the services available from the Languages Unit:

- translation of confidential documents
- interpreting
- safety documentation
- technical literature
- Transport Emergency Cards
- language training.

Naturally, there were some initial linguistic barriers. For example, there was a danger of the project inducing its own specialised form of 'Franglais' which would be understood only by those closely involved.

A key ingredient was the fact that the language service was recognised as accessible and approachable over a whole range of language-related issues. It is quite acceptable and tolerable to have some doors open for dialogue while other doors remain closed for the privacy of translation. It is this interactive dialogue with the user which is the best marketing tool of all. Other marketing techniques include a willingness to cross boundaries and disciplines within the language service area and a small brochure describing the services which are on offer.

CONCLUSION

The advance notes of a forthcoming conference which will examine corporate language policy in European companies state that 'in the 1990s a company without a corporate language policy will be as out of step and at as much disadvantage as one today without a corporate marketing policy'. Within my own organisation we still have a long way to go and this fact is clearly recognised. Nonetheless, I believe that we have made a good start not only in developing the role of the 'language co-ordinator' but that, in so doing, we have also enabled the language service to get alongside its users and to begin to become a key member of the 'business team'. Further, since we use a large number of external suppliers, the second partnership is with the truly professional practitioners from the various sectors of the language service industry.

Firms may often sub-contract the actual physical transport of their goods to road haulage companies but they will still retain their in-house transport experts to ensure a high quality service. The day may yet come when more British organisations recognise the value of expert, in-house language services on a scale which matches some of the existing models in continental western Europe. One positive step along the way could well be the emergence of the 'language co-ordinator' as a perceived role.

I think that a translation service *per se* is necessarily a backroom service. However, I believe that it can function more effectively and to the greater benefit of all concerned if there is some form of overlapping dialogue with its users and if it is not perceived as a largely separate entity.

We often talk of 'educating the user' and, by supplementing the service with other language-related functions (for example, language training), it may well be possible to achieve a more informed and involved use of the translation service by customers. Such additional functions will, I hope:

- involve a dialogue with users
- enable users to 'think languages'
- respond to the many other foreign language requirements of an organisation.

We all hope that British industry will enable more people to become members of the 'Institute of Overall Linguists'.

In-house training for translators

John D. Graham

Head of Central Translation Services, Mannesmann Demag, Duisburg, Germany

INTRODUCTION

In late 1970s and early 1980s, translation services were complaining about the standard of graduates coming into the profession. At the same time, the universities were complaining that there was no feedback from trade and industry. To resolve these differences, an analysis was made of the requirements to be met by graduates entering into service in translation departments. The results of these preliminary analyses began to take form towards the end of 1981. From these beginnings, a professional profile for translators and interpreters coming into the profession was drawn up. This in turn led to a conference in Cologne in 1983, which gave birth to the co-ordination committee *Praxis und Lehre*.

From 1983 until 1985, this committee met several times per year with their efforts culminating in a memorandum which was addressed both to the practitioners and the trainers. This is a long-term project. Copies of the memorandum are available in German and English, translations into Russian and Spanish to follow. Some parts of this memorandum have already been implemented.

Another way to cope with the problem was to institute a form of continuing training for translators and interpreters.

IN-HOUSE TRANSLATORS – THE REQUIREMENT FOR IN-HOUSE TRAINING

The only corporations which can afford to have their own in-house translators are major companies, multinationals, and those of international standing and/or those with a high percentage of dealings with specific countries. This constellation, however, is a mixed blessing for the translator. The larger the company is, the more diversified the range of products will be. In addition, a great many of the products will become inventions, i.e. their nomenclature is a company-internal matter and the corresponding foreign language designations will have to be coined by the company's own translators in conjunction with representatives and agents in the countries concerned. Another disadvantage of large companies is that they tend to be complex in structure and the individual employee has less and less chance of gaining a general overview. [1]

On top of all this, technology is in a state of constant change. Commercial procedures and methods are extended, supplemented and amended constantly in the course of time. In other words, the status quo now need not be the same as the status quo of 5 or 10 years ago or in 5 or 10 years' time. It has to be admitted that no university or institute of higher education can possibly train student translators and interpreters in every technical, specialised and commercial aspect which they are likely to meet during their subsequent careers. [1] As Leo Hickey so appropriately states, a translator must never be wrong; he need not always be right; the difference between the two may be critical. [2]

Mannesmann Demag is an internationally known and respected company in the heavy mechanical engineering sector, split up into various divisions and product ranges and with subsidiaries in various countries. This covers a wide range of products and services. In conjunction with our training department, we devised a course of continuing training for the translators within the central translation services to acquaint them with all the commercial and technical aspects involved in the day-to-day business of the company and with relation to each product group. This scheme was introduced in 1982 and my first report on the scheme was presented in Mons in 1982. [1]

New translators often arrive from their training institute firmly convinced that they will receive a course of instruction in the company's products, etc. before they actually enter the department. This policy was discussed and evaluated and we finally decided that this was not a viable proposition. The complexity of the technology involved is too much for even a qualified engineer to grasp in the course of several years. The commercial aspects, the legal aspects and all the accounting procedures involved would require another several years to cover in any depth. Consequently, it was decided to introduce each newcomer into the existing and on-going continuing training course. Since the course itself is almost self-perpetuating, everything will be covered in detail at some time or another.

As reported in the proceedings of the International Association Business and Language annual conference held in Mons, Belgium in 1982, [1] the course we finally agreed upon was structured to reflect the logical sequence of events. The major intention here was to instruct the translator in the basic essentials of the subject matter or discipline involved by giving emphasis to points of particular importance and making clear the differences between similar and dissimilar systems. In addition, we respected the traditional boundaries in German industry between commercial and technical activities.

COMMERCIAL ACTIVITIES

The activities of any major company begin at the field marketing stage. The procedures will differ depending on the product: capital goods, customised products or integrated plants will require different treatment to series products. From feasibility studies through the invitation to tender to expiry of the guarantee period with all the ramifications and contractual obligations involved is a formidable field of activity. (For those interested in a detailed presentation of the steps and stages involved, there are two excellent articles in existence, one by Johannes van Kruijssen[3] and one by Alois Plein.[4])

To give a very brief idea of the difficulties encountered, let us briefly examine the differences between guarantee, guaranty and warranty, which are not as easy as they sound.[5]

Guarantee

A written statement assuring that something is of stated quantity, quality, content or benefit, or that it will perform as advertised for a specified period of time. In some cases all or part of the purchaser's money will be refunded if the item fails to meet the terms of the guarantee (money-back guarantee).

Guaranty

A contract, agreement or undertaking involving three parties:

1. The guarantor agrees to see that the performance of
2. the guarantee is fulfilled according to the terms of the contract, agreement, or undertaking.
3. The creditor is the party to benefit by the performance.

Warranty

A promise by a seller (vendor) that the product or property being sold is as represented. The warranty is normally presented with the items sold.

In the early lectures, various types of contract were discussed by specialists from the various departments concerned. These included purchase contracts, co-operation contracts, consortium contracts, master agreements, confidentiality agreements, licensing agreements, assembly and erection agreements, counter-purchasing agreements, repair contracts, joint venture agreements, co-operation agreements, etc. Even a brief survey of the validity period for contract bonds serves as an indication of the niceties involved (Figure 1).

The problems encountered here then throw up further special considerations in the field of financing, loans, credits, securities, insurances, taxes, subsidies and surety. There are, indeed, any number of different insurances, financing methods (depending on the country involved – state enterprise countries have to be dealt with in a manner differing from developing or newly industrialising countries).

Terms and conditions of payment begin with financing of manufacture for large-scale orders with quick procurement of liquid funds and coverage of all risks. They take the form, for example, of cash payment conditions and loan payment conditions. The various modes of payment are then discussed in detail including such aspects as due dates, interests, retention money, etc. The various forms of securities and sureties including currency fluctuation risks, customs and import

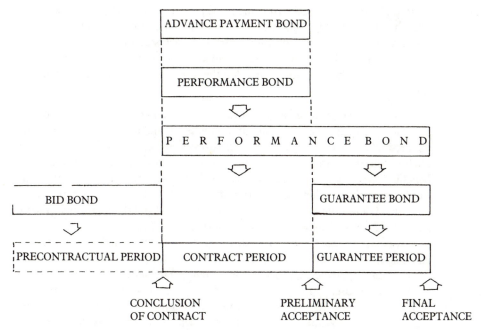

Figure 1. Validity period for contact bonds

duties, and insurance conditions are then covered to round off the picture. The differences in tax forms and the taxes themselves differ from country to country and must be considered individually. [1]

Having dealt with the commercial and legal limits within which the company operates, our training scheme goes on to deal with the procedures for processing an order. The co-ordination work involved at the product stage is followed up by completion of the order and contract documentation, receipt of the appropriate payments, progressing, penalties, hand-over/take-over of documentation, matching price and delivery periods to new customer demands, ensuring appropriate provisions for detectable risks, etc. of the commercial side running in parallel with the technical procedures. Order negotiations, hand-over discussions, progressing, customer contacts, design documents, purchasing, materials disposition, production planning, receipt of goods, control, testing, documentation, despatch and assembly. In this way, the overall bird's eye view is gained. (Many of the specialists lapsed into anecdotes to illustrate the complexity of the tasks involved and, as we all know, these anecdotes tend to be a good means of retaining the information we have just received.)

TECHNICAL ACTIVITIES

On the technical side, we dealt with the general basics such as the materials involved, drawings, parts lists and manufacturing processes. Attention was paid to

SI units and basic technical terms, the principles of physics, dynamics, mechanics and chemistry, to highlight the properties and idiosyncrasies of the various processes for producing steel. Such subsidiary fields as surface treatment, heat treatment, hydraulics, pneumatics, welding, etc. were discussed in detail.

At this point, the programme itself left the realms of theory and entered into the various product fields.

To sum up, the object we had in mind was to cut down the amount of time the translator had to spend researching subject matter. Familiarity with the subject and the products involved increases the translator's knowledge and thereby raises the quality of his or her work. The training scheme, on the other hand also offered the benefit that contact was established between the translators on the one hand and the various specialists within the company divisions, works and departments on the other hand. The scheme itself was introduced in 1980 and the report presented in Mons 1982 was still at a highly theoretical stage. [1]

Obviously, as was to be expected, the translators welcomed this course with enthusiasm. What we did not expect, however, was the positive reaction shown by the specialist departments who took part, providing the speakers and specialists for the various lectures in the programme. At the same time, some of the speakers, whilst crystallising their own thoughts on their own functions even spotted anomalies in the existing sequence of events which have now led to corrections being made to the procedures involved. Another spin-off has been that the translators who took part have gained in stature and experience since then.

At that time, we insisted that the course should follow the natural and logical sequence of events covering the entire process from receipt of the enquiry through to expiry of the guarantee period. It was intended to be a deliberate combination of theory and practice and, to date, has involved a few hours on one morning per week, depending upon subject, location and speaker. These lectures are followed by a hands-on visit to the workshop, etc., involved. In 1982, I reported that this is a very great financial strain, but the rewards had already proven to be significant. Obviously, such an ambitious training scheme could not have been started at all without the active support of the board of directors, the technical training staff and the specialists from the departments concerned. We owe them a debt of gratitude for a courageous decision and hope that this debt is being repaid in the form of better translations of higher quality and within a shorter time.

During the steel crisis of 1983/4, we had to abandon our training scheme. This was a serious blow to us at the time. However, in the course of time, we were able to recommence and have now repeated the entire commercial side because of the implications of the Single European Market. In the meantime, those involved in the training scheme from the beginning had given a great deal of thought to the presentation they made in the first series. They have thought the matter over again, structured their thoughts and updated the information available. This has led to a much better presentation involving charts, slides, overhead slides, etc. In addition, they have begun to appreciate the difficulties of transferring their highly specialised fields of information into another language. In the new series, these speakers have started giving definitions of the various types of loans for example, the various types of insurance, the variety of taxes, etc. On the technical side, the head of technical training gave a series of lectures on the new symbols and new fits in modern drawing practice involving computer-aided drawing. For example, modern drawings cannot be read using the old conventional symbols. The modern system is simple but highly different. There are new methods of measuring, for example. Old methods are incapable of measuring various configurations whereas the new methods now cover these exceptions. The head of technical training also gave an extremely interesting lecture on NC (numerical control) machines, CNC (computerised numerical control) machines, and new production engineering methods, involving visits to the workshop.

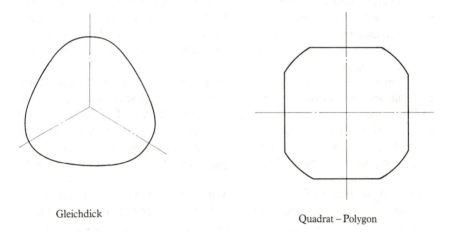

Gleichdick   Quadrat – Polygon

Figure 2. Polygon-profile

One interesting point which arose at this stage is shown in Figure 2. This shows a modern development in positive transmission whereby shafts are no longer round but are polygonal. Polygonal shaft connections are shaft connections with a high degree of centering accuracy. In comparison with keyed connections, these polygonal profiles can cope with higher torques. We are not quite sure what to call them at present but it looks as though equilateral and quadratic polygons are going to be the result.

Some speakers preferred to give their lectures in their own departments or workshops using examples taken from the daily run-of-the-mill work. Some, regarding translators as some kind of exotic plant pitched the level of approach far too low, following the old adage that you should speak *loudly* and *slowly* and *simply* to children, animals and foreigners.

The translators and interpreters in my department are now highly enthusiastic about this training scheme and no form of pressure has to be applied for them to attend. The questions they raise at the end of a lecture are often extremely important to help them clarify the subject matter in their own minds but, as a spin-off product, have also indicated to the speakers that translators can do much more than translate, they can actually think as well.

TERMINOLOGY

There is no way whatsoever in which a translation can be completed without research into terms, subject matter or some other aspects. In view of the fact that most of the terms, procedures, etc. involved were the company's own invention, it was recognised at a very early stage that the terminology had to be discussed with the specialists within the company and then with our representative abroad to arrive at an acceptable translation equivalent. To this end, one translator in the English group was asked to start building a terminology bank. It sounded like a good idea at the time but was a mammoth task with very little assistance and no experience to use as a foundation.

It soon became clear that the only sensible way to proceed with terminology, especially in-house terminology, was to research following scientific principles. At first we joined up with the Bundessprachenamt in Hürth. This gave us a solid footing and enabled us to gain quite a lot of information on procedures and methods. In 1976 we learned of TEAM run by Siemens AG through their main-frame computer in Munich. This was a gigantic step forward and we soon joined TEAM as members.

In 1980, we then decided to intensify our co-operation with TEAM for the language combination English-German. The last print-out from the Siemens computer gave us 1,800 pages of terms with definitions and references and the equivalents in the other language in each direction, German-English and English-German. In the meantime, the terminology section has grown to include French, Spanish and Portuguese.

It must be emphasised that we are building up a terminology bank, not a glossary or an in-house 'dictionary'. The terms researched and classified are actual terms from everyday documents passing through our hands and refer to concrete instances. Naturally, of course, we do a lot of prophylactic terminology research. When you find one term, you find left and right of it another term or terms which are worth noting. It is not the general consensus of opinion that terminologists should note every term that crosses their path, but this is the system we follow. Any term in any text which requires research or any other particular treatment is noted and held on file even if only in one language, pending discovery of the equivalent in the other language(s).

Another school of thought says you should deal with one complete subject-matter field in one go. We do, also, occasionally follow this practice. However, Herbert Bucksch, a well-known compiler of dictionaries in West Germany, claims that even an extensive search through the literature available on any subject will only cover about 60 per cent of the technical terms involved. The time and effort required to fill in the remaining 40 per cent is disproportionately high. As a consequence, the first editions of such dictionaries tend to be less than satisfactory because they are incomplete, but they do improve with each reissue.

We tend to look for a definition, explanation or drawing to define the content of the concept involved. Like the Bundessprachenamt, we are against the translator writing down his or her own definition without having it checked by a specialist, and under no circumstances should the translator make any attempt to translate the definition from one language into another. This is a highly questionable practice which, in our opinion, provides no satisfactory results.

The difficulties which beset the translator are brilliantly described by Jean Datta[6] in which she says that whereas Arabic has a whole collection of words for kinds of camel, English looks upon the beast as alien. A camel is a camel – unless it is a dromedary. Similar difficulties also arise in technical texts with certain terms (e.g. 'control'). We place primary emphasis upon terms which are new, newly coined, with a special meaning, or terms which only have significance in one language (e.g. in accounting, the German terms *Lastenausgleich* or *Rechnungsabgrenzungsposten*, which have no direct equivalents in English).

CONCLUSION

The immediate benefits of combining our terminology service with our continuing training scheme are:

- Uniform terminology is employed by all translators so that large-scale rush jobs can actually be split up among several translators with no disparities in terminology (in style, yes).
- The time required by a newcomer to the department to acclimatise himself or herself to the processes, terminology and procedures within the company is reduced from approximately five to two years for beginners. This provides much more job satisfaction and makes economic employment of the newcomer possible at a much earlier stage without the need for a 'babysitter'.

We are now in the process of linking our stocks of terminology in the various languages, based on the German stock so that the base term need only be defined, clarified and entered once. The other language groups can then build on this foundation. (It also offers the possibility of adding to the term where necessary or correcting any possible errors – even terminologists are human!) In view of the fact that we are constantly being asked to do cross translations from say French into English or Spanish into Russian, this facility greatly improves the quality of the translations and also speeds up the translation procedure. My major problem here is how to finance these schemes.

Life looks like becoming more difficult for us as well in view of the Single European Market and its ramifications – product liability to name but one!

REFERENCES

[1]   GRAHAM, J.D.: *International Association for Business and Language, Proceedings of the annual conference 1982*, Mons, Belgium.

[2]   HICKEY, Leo: 'A basic maxim for practical translation', in *The Incorporated Linguist*, Vol. 24, No. 2, Spring 1985, pp 106–109.

[3]   VAN KRUIJSSEN, J.: 'Die Übersetzung im Grossanlagengeschäft', in *Mitteilungsblatt für Dolmetscher und Übersetzer*, Vol. 16, No. 2, March 1970, pp 1–3.

[4]   PLEIN, A.: 'Aufgaben, Probleme und Verantwortung des angestellten Übersetzers in der freien Wirtschaft', in *Mitteilungsblatt für Dolmetscher und Übersetzer*, Vol. 33, No. 5, pp 12–15.

[5]   ROSENBERG, J.N: *A dictionary of business and management.*

[6]   DATTA, J.: 'A camel is a camel – unless it's a dromedary', in *Language Monthly*, September 1986, p 36.

Session 1: Report of discussion

Rapporteur: Heather Wheeller, Assistant Manager, Translation Section, Lloyds Bank Plc

Jane Taylor of the University of Manchester asked Doug Embleton how far a translation service is reactive and how far can it (or should it?) show future need within the company? Doug Embleton replied that although it is largely reactive the translation service can extend itself and be ready for future translation needs and so a little of both is the answer. Most of the work is passed down the line in ICI but as the language unit carries out surveys and questionnaires to ascertain language needs within the company it does have the possibility of feeding messages up the line.

Catriona Picken then asked John Graham about the staffing of the terminology section. Was there still only one individual as he said in his talk? John Graham replied that the original terminologist had now retired but the work had been extended to French, Spanish and Portuguese. They are working on Dutch and Russian. There are now two full-time terminologists and three part-timers. Their work is fed to them by the translators.

Gerald Beck, freelance translator, asked Doug Embleton about his comment on the elimination of proofreading referred to in his talk. Mr Embleton said that some stages of proofreading were being cut out because terminology was being refined all the time and that what he meant was that more work was being produced on floppy disk, being proofread and then interfaced with the typesetting operation with the result that some stages in the proofreading could be eliminated.

Martina Marchinton, freelance translator and interpreter, London, asked how John Graham and Mannesmann imparted the required engineering knowledge to a newly-recruited staff translator with no technical background. Are company brochures and factory visits sufficient as background information? Or should the translators not have an engineering degree? John Graham replied yes, and that they should have seven degrees, in engineering, law, computer studies, etc . . . but that the people with all these qualifications were not willing to work for the salaries Mannesmann offered them. He said Hildesheim business school had developed a new course which was theoretical but at least gives people an idea of what they are letting themselves in for. However, the knowledge gained in the department and in the company is usually enough to guide people through most of the problems they encounter. The two- or three-hour lectures held on Tuesday mornings helped in training and the company videos can be taken out and watched by anyone in the department to help them get some knowledge of the product or service.

Ms Marchinton then asked a further question. Clients very often expect translation to be presented in a ready-to-print form which may involve using a desktop publishing system. She asked both John Graham and Doug Embleton whether they give their staff translators training in desktop publishing. John Graham said that in Germany worker representation was very strong and very active. Job descriptions were very tightly drawn up and if he asked his translators to use a new system such as desktop publishing they would demand re-training and new job descriptions. There was also the factor that the translation department is a service department, and service departments do not need new things, after all they have dictionaries. He said that the translation department is a cost factor although within the company it should be seen as a value factor. The answer is, he feels, to transform the department. In Krupps, for example, the translation department has been transformed into the documentation department and can charge five times as much for the finished documentation than for a 'straight' translation, so the company is willing to make the investment. He also said he gives his freelances the opportunity to take part in the training schemes he runs.

Doug Embleton said that in his languages unit any individual customer's job is always the most urgent. It is very difficult to convey the need for desktop publishing or terminologists. The unit has strong liaison with freelances on an interpersonal level. Each job is microfiched and referenced on a database. The recent merger of areas in the organisation resulted in 15,000–18,000 hard copy translations being sent to them in tea-chests. They rescued them, microfiched them and gave them new translation titles. As a result, ICI Australia and ICI Canada could now request the translation of a document and it could usually be found easily and readily. Duplication was also cut down. However, there was very rarely the justification to support the cost of a desktop publishing system.

Kirsty Buxbom, translation manager of Rank Xerox asked why the translation department did not set up as a profit centre rather than a cost centre. John Graham said that as a cost centre their costs must be covered and translations are charged out to the departments requesting them. All sorts of costing schemes have been tried. They try to charge for urgency and any job of over 1,000 words in a day is given an urgency surcharge, or if the sequence in which work is done is changed in any way, this is charged. Extra research is charged for as well. He said that their costs were visible because they are a cost centre. The disadvantage of charging for everything is that if a small department requests a translation which is given a high charge, their budget cannot be expanded to cover much translation work or else one translation shows up as a disproportionately large amount of their budget.

Ms Buxbom asked a second question about charging freelance translators for taking part in in-house training programmes, as surely it was in the company's interest to receive a quality translation that reflects product knowledge and should not the translators therefore be paid to take part in the product training? John Graham had said that not many freelance translators took advantage of his training talks. In his reply he said that translators were not charged for attending the training courses he arranged and he regretted that they did not want to attend but the translators felt they had no time to spare as they were not earning whilst attending, and time is money.

Session 2: Technology

Chaired by Pamela Mayorcas

Paperless documents

John Murphy

Special Projects Manager, InterMedia Graphic Systems Ltd

For most organisations electronic document transfer is going to become the norm over the next few years. This is because sending, receiving or updating documents in this way is safer, cheaper and faster than the old paper methods of re-keying and typesetting or photocopying. This is especially true for text where the general rule today is to keep all text in electronic form for editing right up to the last minute before printing. The systems used to do this will rapidly increase in sophistication in the near future.

In broad terms the two methods which are of interest here are communications and disk transfer.

COMMUNICATIONS

With the current audience in mind, with people working off-site or at home, this would mean having a personal computer and modem and receiving and sending text over the telephone lines. This is very easy to set up and would normally be instigated by the client who would define and agree the methods, procedures and word processing formats of the operation. The client may even offer to supply the computer, modem and word processing software and pay the telephone charges.

The disadvantages are that the speed of data transfer is quite low, and that some organisations have difficulty setting things up in this way – especially if they do not have other people working off-site using a similar system (technical authors or company reps). Security is also a concern that is raised (hackers could get into the company's computer systems!). However, when properly set up with the proper controls and the right equipment at both ends, these arrangements work well.

DISK TRANSFER

This is where the client prefers to be supplied with the work on a particular type of disk, with a particular type of file or word processing format. Generally this is because the client has a word processing system or an electronic publishing system which needs data presented in this way. The best solution is, of course, to use exactly the same word processor but that may not always be possible or preferable.

There are a number of solutions and considerations and I have detailed them below with some comments. However, whatever the agreed method you should always, repeat always, test before submitting live data even if everything looks straightforward. Untested and untried word processing features have a habit of becoming impossible as deadlines approach.

1. Find out what kind of files your own word processor can produce and make some samples. You should be able to produce a variety of files other than the usual one. See below for PRINT FILES, ASCII, DCA and ODA.
2. Describe to the client the equipment and disks you normally work with, and ask if any of the files you produce can be used instead and offer to provide samples. Sometimes a file you can prepare with your system will be acceptable – even if the size is different to the one first mentioned.
3. If this fails or you cannot get answers you understand, ask your clients for a sample disk in the format they want you to supply, and a typical file and its printout. Give these to a bureau together with some samples from your own machine and describe the potential job. Ask for prices, timings, etc., and get them to do a test conversion of one of your files so that you can then test with your own client. I strongly suggest you do this even if it seems you are bothering the client unduly – the client should not think so, and anyway it looks professional. Real and expensive disasters can be averted at this stage. The bureau should be able to advise if you could do this work on your own machine – but remember they do not know all the machines or word processors intimately.
4. Tell the client of your conversion arrangements. The client may then be able to appreciate and offer advice on the unexpected or unusual instead of complaining.

GLOSSARY AND HINTS

PRINT FILES Usually acceptable if the client can read the disk in the first place, but only in the sense that the file will probably not contain any underlining or emboldening. Usually created after the question on your word processor 'PRINT TO DISK?'.

ASCII FILES Similar to PRINT FILES and often taken as the same. These also do not contain any underlining and emboldening, nor usually any indentation or margin changes – strictly words and spaces. Curiously, often more acceptable than PRINT FILES in spite of their appearance. Produced at commands such as 'SAVE ASCII?'.

DCA Document Content Architecture. An IBM standard, it does preserve presentation such as underlining, emboldening, tabs, indents, centering, etc. Unfortunately, sometimes known as 'RFT' or Revisable Form Text files. Look in the manual or take advice. Can be produced by many modern PC word processors such as Displaywrite, Samna, Word, etc. The client may only know it as 'RFT' or 'Displaywrite RFT'.

ODA
Office Document Architecture. The international version of DCA, supposedly going to be adopted by everyone. Not yet implemented but worth watching out for as it will become available on mini and mainframe computers and publishing systems before the smaller word processors catch up.

CHARACTER SETS

Many modern word processors allow the easy keying of other (known as Non-UK) character sets, but please be aware that setting up systems to handle them is sometimes very tricky and time-consuming. This is an area where testing and agreement are absolutely vital. A final observation I would like to make is that when organisations become familiar with an outside supplier interacting with their own in-house computer systems either through communications or disk transfer, they become less likely to consider competition for that service.

On that note, good luck for the future.

Telecommuting – The work pattern of the future

Sue Halbert

CPS Professional Services, ICL

INTRODUCTION

ICL is the leading UK-owned systems supplier. ICL is also one of the pioneers and leading practitioners of 'telecommuting' – also referred to as 'networking', home-working, remote working, distance working and now teleworking, which means employing staff who work remotely from their direct management with no direct daily supervision but with the aid of Information Technology products. In ICL's case all the telecommuters, including myself, work from home. This form of working is becoming increasingly common in the UK – there will be a predicted 4 million of us by 1995 – and, of course, it is particularly suitable for translation work. Many of you perhaps already work from home yourselves.

My paper will cover:

– why there is such a trend towards telecommuting
– the ICL experience
– the major issues
– the benefits to both organisations and individuals.

WHY IS TELECOMMUTING GROWING?

Telecommuting is growing, firstly, because of economic and social trends:

– skills and labour shortages, worsening in the 1990s in the UK. The so-called 'demographic time-bomb' means that employers are developing flexible working options, such as home working, to encourage more women into their employ
– high cost of office accommodation, particularly in the inner cities
– high cost of commuting in the South-East
– stress of commuting on over-crowded roads and railways
– the UK's North-South divide. The prosperous South has plenty of work and expensive housing, while the depressed North has cheaper housing and less work. Southern-based companies now recruit people in the North and establish them as 'telecommuters'

- in the US the trend is being driven by the 'Green factor'. In Southern California, for example, companies with over 100 employees must file plans to show how they are cutting down on car usage, and telecommuting is one solution.
- finally, 'lifestyle': staff demand more leisure time.

Secondly, of course, there is the technological progress which has made it all possible. Small personal computers, photocopiers and fax machines are now widely available and are relatively cheap and compact; and, of course, we also have electronic messaging and mail services, teleconferencing, message switching and the ansaphone. All these make home-based workers as accessible as their office-based colleagues. Of course 'telecommuting' can work extremely well without all the high-tech – ICL have been operating in this way very successfully since 1969 when all we had was a telephone and postal system!

The ICL home-based unit which I represent is called CPS Professional Services. It has been in operation for over 18 years, and has over 300 staff, nationwide. All staff and managers are home-based, and enjoy full employee status. We can work part-time or full-time as we wish, or as personal circumstances dictate. The unit is supported by four on-site staff, who handle our administration and equipment supplies, etc.

Within ICL we operate as a systems house providing programmers, systems designers, technical authors and project managers and consultants to internal ICL projects and to ICL's customers. All our 'telecommuters' are highly skilled professional staff who can, because of their experience, work extremely effectively with no supervision.

The criteria for joining the scheme are very strict: technically we expect individuals to have a minimum of five years' experience, be technically very competent, and commercially aware. We also require them to have strong personal qualities, in particular to have high levels of self discipline, be self-sufficient, self-motivating, have bags of initiative and above all be flexible. Domestically, we insist that they have a quiet area of the home, with a telephone, which they can dedicate to their work, have adequate child-minding facilities if relevant and be pretty mobile. Most of our home workers have to visit site at least once per week.

Originally all our staff were recruited from within ICL. Nearly 20 years later, the picture looks very different; 45 per cent were originally employed by ICL, while the remaining 55 per cent come from our users, competitors and freelances attracted in by the benefits of being an employee. This clearly shows how ICL has benefited from its home-working policy in that it has been able to attract and recruit highly competent IT professionals into the company. Last year alone we had nearly 600 unsolicited applicants to join our unit. The signs are that we shall double this in 1989.

The terms of employment are broadly exactly the same as those for on-site staff. We have the same grading and salary structure and are entitled to all company benefits including holiday pay, sick pay, maternity pay, pensions and cars, plus health insurance for senior staff and managers. The specific clauses relating to the home-working state that our place of work is home, travelling time and expenses are paid from home, we have standard contract hours and are paid benefits on a pro-rata basis. We are paid for hours worked and in the event that no work is available then a retainer is paid.

Control is achieved by employing very rigorous management control procedures. We employ the same techniques that any well managed organisation uses. The main difference is that we absolutely have to do it, formally and properly, because of the remoteness of staff and management.

Planning and scheduling are carefully done at the start of each project. Objectives and schedules are written down and used for subsequent reviewing. Staff agree to objectives and are accountable thereafter. Progress reporting is formal and strictly adhered to, as are standards and procedures for ensuring quality of output. Regular feedback and appraisals ensure that CPS systems and procedures are relevant and useful. We cannot afford to be casual. We have discovered that nothing exposes weak management more quickly than working in this way. However, we have not reached this well organised state without encountering a few obstacles along the way. Some of the issues we have experienced and addressed are as follows.

Timescales

Having all our staff and management remote from each other initially caused a slowing down of progress and longer elapsed times. Technology has changed all that, since staff are now online to mainframe computers giving instant input and results, and both staff and management use electronic mail and messaging via ICL PCs for communication. Managers use local secretaries for a few hours each week to leave them free to manage, and in addition, we make extensive use of technical productivity aids. Finally, the simple telephone answering machine with which all staff are equipped means more efficient and better planned communication.

Training

Keeping skills up to date has always been a priority but it is difficult for off-site staff to attend residential courses. We have overcome this through the use of distance learning techniques, of videos, audios and workbooks, as well as 'modularised courses', and tailored courses in off-site management techniques for instruction in telephone techniques, etc.

Social isolation

To overcome the social isolation which home-based staff often experience we have taken the following measures:

- regular newsletters in various forms
- regular management contact by phone
- contact through work itself, team meetings, etc.
- social events, local, regional and national throughout the year
- mentorship of new recruits.

Equipment

The employees need equipment in order to do the work. This in turn presents its own set of problems since repairing equipment in remote locations can take time, and large quantities of manuals and equipment can create storage problems, especially in small houses. To solve these problems we set up a support network for kit and use microfiche and electronic media for documentation wherever possible. Fortunately, the problem is now less serious, because equipment is becoming much more compact.

Staff issues

As with any organisation, having good staff is the recipe for success. We try to ensure this by getting it right at the start by rigorous selection procedures. We also try to identify poor performers as early as possible through regular reviews, early evidence of work and regular contact. It is important to understand the individual's personal circumstances and allocate suitable work. Lastly, we provide counselling services to overcome personal or work-related problems such as time-management, etc.

Benefits

The benefits to ICL of the home-based working scheme are very real. We are able to retain and attract highly skilled staff who would be unable to work in a conventional environment and have found that this applies not only to women with young families, but also, for instance, to those with invalid dependents, disabled staff, those undertaking further education, plus those who wish to work in this way to improve the quality of their lives, etc. Home as a workplace is highly conducive to work which results in high levels of productivity and the staff are highly committed and loyal. The traditional overheads of employing staff, such as rent, rates, heating, etc. do not apply. In the long run, the operation is therefore much more profitable. The scheme not only delays attrition but reduces it as well. Staff do leave the scheme but only at a rate of about five per cent per year.

The benefits are not just one-way. The benefits to staff are that they do not suffer the disadvantages of a career break with the resultant loss of knowledge and confidence and can enjoy continuous career development through a period when they are unable to work in a conventional environment. Staff enjoy flexibility as to when they work and for how many hours. And, of course, a house move does not necessitate a job move. Staff have the opportunity to transfer back to on-site work should they wish, when their personal circumstances permit.

To finish I would like to say that in our experience teleworking can be a very effective and beneficial way to employ staff. The techniques developed prove that this style of work is suitable to many other categories of job outside the Information Technology industry. With committed management, well-selected staff, good practices and training, many other organisations will no doubt successfully implement similar schemes over the coming years. To assist this ICL/CPS now offer remote working management consultancy. Please contact Sue Halbert on 024 028 359 to discuss these services.

Session 2: Report of discussion

Rapporteur: Julie Slade, Translation Manager, Digital Equipment

Regarding John Murphy's paper, Robert Clark commented that there are various alternatives to bureau disk conversions for PC-compatible machines and well-known word processors. He offered the following alternatives:

1. various sizes of disk drive can be fitted to a PC (if that is what is used) and the files copied
2. two computers with different disk formats can be connected by a cable and files transferred using software
3. a modem can be used to send files from one type of computer to another
4. if the two computers are not using the same word processing (WP) software it may be necessary to transfer files via the ASCII format, but if the same WP software is used the files should transfer perfectly.

He commented on the difficulty with the widely used Amstrad PCW series posed by the Locoscript software used. This does not exist for other computers, so Locoscript files must be converted to ASCII before transfer to another type of computer. This means that a bureau must also be used for dedicated word processors, such as those made by Xerox, Wang, etc. John Murphy replied that ASCII conversion on PCs is not always satisfactory. The trend is towards more people having their own machine but success in disk conversion will depend upon the degree of sophistication available.

Sono Barnes from the Japan Communication Service, New Zealand, asked John Murphy what sorts of computer software were available to accommodate the needs for translating between European and non-European languages. She also asked whether there was sufficient demand for translation and interpreting between these languages in Europe to justify the cost of developing software. John Murphy replied that there is a company in Singapore which specialises in this and cited Thai as an example, but said that he did not have any further details.

Iain MacKenzie asked Sue Halbert whether ICL felt they were getting value for money from 'teleworkers' as compared with freelances. What are the advantages of using teleworkers? Sue Halbert replied that the advantages for the employer are that the staff are committed to the company and they can work on sensitive prototype products where external contractors would not be used. In commercial terms, employee costs are cheaper than freelance rates and their skills can be redeployed on the next contract. She also commented that in ICL teleworkers were initially freelance because it was an experimental scheme. Only after six years when there were 50–60 people did ICL make 'honest women' of them.

Pamela Mayorcas said that it was interesting to consider whether one day translators would be regarded as being as important to a company as programmers and analysts.

Christine Lund-Alderin of the Finnish Translators and Interpreters Association asked Sue Halbert what percentage of homeworkers were women. Sue Halbert replied that the figure was 90 per cent. More men are now applying to join the scheme, but originally all participants were women.

Roger Fletcher commented that a computer magazine recently suggested that the greatest obstacle to telecommuting is the fact that telephone lines in rural areas are above ground and subject to interference from snow and high winds. He asked whether this had been a problem in Sue Halbert's experience. Sue Halbert agreed that the quality of telephone lines was a problem but much work is done offline. Online work was carried out overnight.

Barbara Laughlin asked Sue Halbert whether any allowance was made for child care costs in pay rates or whether the company provided subsidies? Sue Halbert said this did not happen because computer professionals could afford to pay for child care. The situation could change but at present child care costs are directly taxable. She also commented that ICL is involved in the Women into Information Technology campaign and one of the aims of this campaign is to secure child care provision.

Session 3: Training

Chaired by Jane Taylor

University versus in-service training

Hugh Keith

Heriot-Watt University, Edinburgh

(Despite the author's membership of the ITI Education and Training Committee, any opinions expressed in the following paper are entirely his own.)

INTRODUCTION

At the first ITI conference in 1987 the 'education and training' session included descriptions of the activities of the applied language departments at the NIHE (National Institute for Higher Education) in Dublin and Bradford University. In 1988 Michael Croft of the postgraduate course at Bath University widened the discussion to include a general assessment of the situation of the training of professional linguists in the UK. [1]

It is my intention in this paper to take up and discuss some of the points Michael Croft made. I shall examine training of translators in general, but I will inevitably use the Heriot-Watt course when I cite examples.

LAST YEAR'S DISCUSSIONS

In his 1987 paper Michael Croft mentioned four issues in particular which I consider to be important:

1. He raised the question of whether undergraduate or postgraduate training is the most appropriate for translators.
2. He discussed the question of standards and suggested that maintenance of standards implied the close involvement of the profession in the training and examining processes.
3. In connection with 2 he asked to what extent course planning – both in terms of content and of examination pass-rates – should be related to the needs of the market, in as much as one can determine these.
4. Although he did raise the question of English and word processing skills, he did not look in particular detail at the other skills which need to be acquired on such courses. I shall spend much of this paper considering what the components in a translator training course should be, but I will also keep in mind the more basic matters of principle covered in 1–3 above. In particular – as the title of this paper suggests – I shall be considering whether the

components of translator training which I isolate can be taught at undergraduate or postgraduate level, or whether they should be left to in-service courses.

First, however, it may be useful to look briefly at the situation as it is now. As with most things British, we are faced with a system which has developed fairly haphazardly over the years and presents a sometimes confusing picture. To avoid perpetuating such confusion it is important that a proper overview of the situation should be achieved and it is perhaps an institution such as the ITI which is in the best position to do so and to offer advice and recommendations as to what future developments should be.

THE PRESENT SITUATION

Languages at school

In his introductory remarks to this conference Professor Sager has already mentioned the alarming decline in languages at school level which has taken place over the past 10 years or more. At present 60 per cent of secondary school children give up studying a modern language after the age of 14. The introduction of the common core curriculum may now ensure that one language – usually French – will be taught to age 16 in most schools, but the corollary is that other languages, such as German, Italian and Spanish will decline. There is, moreover, an acute shortage of language teachers at secondary level. This is having a knock-on effect on higher education. Already many undergraduate courses at university level are having to offer *ab initio* courses to students wishing to study languages other than French. This general narrowing of the scope for language study contrasts with the exhortations from educationalists and from industry that we ought to be not only expanding the numbers taking languages to a high level but also broadening the range of languages which are on offer.

Undergraduate courses

At present a number of institutions offer so-called 'applied' language courses at undergraduate level – Ealing, Salford, Bradford, Bath, Heriot-Watt, Aston, etc. In addition, others now offer an element of translation studies in their programme, e.g. Kent, Surrey. One should note here a paradox, however: despite the apparent vocational orientation of such undergraduate courses in Great Britain they still lead to a general, rather than a specific professional qualification. That 70 per cent plus of graduates from Heriot-Watt use their languages professionally after graduating masks the fact that these include not just professional translators and interpreters but also those who go into teaching and those who gain employment in businesses abroad. And it still leaves 20–30 per cent who use their qualification as a basic arts qualification and train subsequently in another area such as banking or accountancy. There would seem to be a traditional expectation in Great Britain that a BA honours degree in an arts subject should provide elements of a general liberal education which serve as a basis for subsequent professional training. This situation contrasts very strongly, for example, with that in the Federal Republic of Germany, where there are separate undergraduate university courses leading to the qualification of Diplom-Übersetzer (or Diplom-Dolmetscher) and one takes an entirely different course of studies if one wishes to become, for example, a teacher.

Postgraduate courses

There are also a number of well-established postgraduate courses – for example at the Polytechnic of Central London, Bradford, Bath, Salford – which offer a vocationally-oriented training taught partly by professional translators and interpreters. Again, however, we are faced with a paradox. One might expect these postgraduate courses to combine with the 'applied' undergraduate courses to form a double structure for the training of translators. One could argue that this would be an ideal system. In reality, however, the postgraduate courses still seem to function largely as 'conversion' courses for people who have taken more traditional undergraduate degrees in modern languages. As such they have an important and necessary function within the system as it is at present.

A further factor related to postgraduate courses is the pessimism expressed by Michael Croft in his paper and shared by many in higher education about the future of such courses in the UK. It should be remembered that the local authorities in England, Wales and Northern Ireland and the Scottish Education Department do not have any statutory obligation to give financial support to students on postgraduate courses, and that it is becoming increasingly difficult for students to acquire such support.

Professional bodies

A final important factor in the present situation is the existence of bodies like the Institute of Linguists and the ITI – both of which have developed new exams with a professional orientation for linguists and are looking at the possibilities of organising short courses for professional linguists in need of acquiring extra skills.

Formal training versus on-the-job training

Finally there is the fact that large numbers of those at present working as translators did not receive any specific vocational training prior to joining the profession but rather learnt their skills on the job. There now seems to be a general consensus that some degree of training prior to joining the profession is desirable. There will, however, probably always remain a certain tension between the principle of institutional training for translators and that of training through job-experience. I will be suggesting below that we need to look more closely at ways of reconciling those two principles.

BDÜ Memorandum 'Praxis und Lehre'. When we consider the above situation it is perhaps useful to look at what is happening in another country in this field. John Graham has already mentioned the Memorandum[2] published in 1986 by a committee of the translators' and interpreters' association in the Federal Republic of Germany, the BDÜ (Bundesverband der Dolmetscher und Übersetzer). The committee brought together teachers and professional linguists and the memorandum set out their views on what the training of translators and interpreters should ideally consist of. It is a document well worth studying and the discussions which led up to its publication are an exercise which we could well go through in this country. At the same time we should be careful about advocating the transferral of the system of one country to another. Great Britain has, as described above, a rather different tradition of higher education from West Germany. Nevertheless, the same basic questions asked by the BDÜ committee could be asked in this country, even if the way the education system responds may be a different one.

Elements in translator training. The basic question posed by the BDÜ committee was: What are the components we would like to see in a translator training course? To this one could add, in the British context: To what extent should/can these be taught at university or polytechnic, and if so, at what level, or should they be taught 'on the job'?

The following elements can be isolated, though the list is probably incomplete:

- mother tongue competence
- foreign-language(s) competence
- translating competence
- subject knowledge
- procedural skills
- practical skills.

The last two categories may need some explanation. The term *procedural skills* refers to processes such as glossary-building, terminology searches, as well as the use of dictionaries, and existing glossaries and databases. The term *practical skills* refers to more basic matters such as typing, word processing, use of dictaphones, fax, electronic mail, etc.

It should be made clear that what one can separate into categories for the purpose of theoretical discussion should not necessarily be kept separate when it comes to the actual training process itself. For example many practical skills can be acquired without large amounts of time being lavished on formal instruction. More importantly it is not necessary, in my opinion, to separate language competence from translation competence in training – once one is beyond a certain threshold (which would need to be defined) the two can be acquired parallel to each other. This is an important point because it touches on Michael Croft's question of whether training should occur at undergraduate or postgraduate level. It is interesting to note that the BDÜ memorandum makes a simple pronouncement on this: 'Die Ausbildung darf nicht durch Sprachdefizite behindert werden' ('The training process should not be hampered by deficiencies in the language competence of the students').

A statement such as this begs the question of where the threshold should be set below which deficiencies in language competence hamper training. It should be noted that what is in question is not what is the ideal level of foreign language competence for a translator, but at what stage in a linguist's development he or she can start learning how to translate in addition to continuing the development of his or her foreign language skills. David Denby of the NIHE, in an intervention during the discussion of Michael Croft's paper at the 1988 conference, made the point that at undergraduate level the acquisition of language skills and the acquisition of translation skills were separate elements, both of which were important. The implication of the BDÜ statement would appear to be that one first teaches the language and then one teaches the translation skills. Taking this approach to its logical conclusion would result in the setting up of a dual system of university training consisting of intensive language study at undergraduate level followed by vocational training at postgraduate level. Leaving aside the question of the feasibility of such a system in the prevailing atmosphere in higher education in Britain, I would challenge the assumption that in the British context this has to be the case. And here I would offer the example of the Heriot-Watt undergraduate course. The structure of the Heriot-Watt course[3] makes it possible to produce linguists at the end of four years who can – and do – move very successfully into careers as professional translators.

THE HERIOT-WATT EXPERIENCE

The changing situation in schools may well force Heriot-Watt to alter its approach in the future, but at present, by carefully selecting candidates on the basis of their examination results at school and by subjecting them to an individual interview to assess not only their motivation and general attitude but also their articulacy in English and their interest in political and cultural affairs, it is possible to select candidates who prove successful on the course.

Language competence

In German – which is my language – teaching concentrates during the first term of the first year on intensive language work, taught exclusively in the language, aimed at lessening any differences there may be between individual students' experience of the language. Then translating starts – while at the same time the basic language teaching continues. During this first year students also follow a course entitled text-analysis. This is more practically oriented than it may sound. While students are initially introduced to a theoretical model of language communication and to some of the terminology of discourse analysis, the course also tries to encourage them to think in very practical terms about what texts are, how they are put together and what the options are which a writer of any text faces.

Students are required to write or rewrite a number of texts themselves during the course. All the texts studied are in English. This course represents in part an attempt to respond to the challenge of what to do about students' mother-tongue skills. It tries to foster a greater awareness of the difference between well-written and badly-written English. Complaints about students' English form a *leitmotiv* in conversations with employers and in discussions with fellow language teachers. It is perhaps the one area where most needs to be done but where the greatest uncertainty reigns. I would suggest that further investigation should be made into precisely what employers mean when they complain about their recruits' English – do they mean spelling and punctuation, or are they referring to more fundamental deficiencies? It may even be in some cases that complaints about employees' English are in fact complaints about their *translation* competence as much as their actual mother-tongue competence. In preparing this paper I contacted two dozen firms which were known to recruit significant numbers of professional linguists. I included a question about English language skills in a questionnaire which I sent them. There seemed to be two different types of response:

– some firms complained of poor spelling and punctuation
– one, however, also pointed out that 'the poor English that is sometimes produced is not usually due to an inadequate command of the language, but the inability to distance themselves from the sentence structures in the foreign text'.

The reluctance to tackle the problem of students' English on university courses is perhaps a legacy from the traditional modern language courses where the emphasis was naturally placed on the foreign language and translation was used largely as a comprehension exercise. Teachers on such courses could legitimately shrug off any responsibility for their students' English and concentrate on teaching the foreign languages. But as soon as teaching aims at the training of professional translators, English assumes central importance. We have, I think, been slow to recognise this.

As far as foreign language skills are concerned one vital element in the training students receive at Heriot-Watt is the year abroad, which is spent not as an English-teaching assistant in a school, but as a full-time student attending classes in a translating and interpreting institute in each of two appropriate countries for the languages being studied. This third year of the course therefore becomes an important part of the general foreign language training of the students, but it occurs parallel to the students' translating activities.

It is interesting to note here an interesting comment made by one of the firms who responded to my questionnaire. Answering the question about deficiencies in English, the firm stated: 'Those who had spent some time abroad were less able to communicate fluently in English. Their English was "contaminated" by phrases, word order, etc. in their foreign language(s).' This might seem to suggest that the need to devote more time and resources to development of students' English increases with their exposure to the foreign language(s). My own experience is not that students' ability to translate well is actually adversely affected by their year abroad, but there would certainly seem to be a difference between the effects of foreign residence on their performance in translating and their performance in interpreting. There is often a spectacular improvement in interpreting competence after the year abroad, as a result of an improved capacity for processing oral language; but there is not necessarily a correspondingly large improvement in translating performance.

Translation competence

Part of the Text Analysis course consists of an introduction to a classification of text types which it is felt may be helpful in deciding what translation strategy to adopt (based on the classification by Reiss[4]). Students are also introduced to the principles and techniques of translation in the second year and given a course in translation theory in their fourth year. More importantly though, even when translation is carried out in the first year of the course – as part of the foreign language teaching programme – an attempt is made to relate it to the professional activity. Thus students are never handed a text and asked to translate it without being told the purpose of the translation – is it for publication, for information only, for the extraction of specific information, etc.?; and the type of client involved – what assumptions can be made about his or her knowledge of the subject, the country, etc.? In the classes discussion inevitably also covers the characteristics of the English equivalent of the particular text type involved. Thus foreign-language learning, cultivation of a greater awareness of English and certain practical aspects of translation competence can all be combined in one activity.

Subject knowledge

It is useful to differentiate between what one might term 'background studies' and actual specialist areas, such as law, medicine, engineering, etc. At Heriot-Watt background studies – the history, politics, social affairs, etc. of the countries concerned – are taught in two different ways. Firstly there are courses in precisely such areas – history in the first year; European studies in the second year; international economy and international organisations in the fourth year. But a 'topic' system is also operated for all language teaching, whereby for a number of weeks all language classes, in both the languages being studied, concentrate on – to take some random examples – environmental issues, political parties, or education. This not only gives the course some internal coherence, but also enables 'cross-fertilisation' to occur from one class to another – particularly where the question of terminology in English is concerned.

Apart from the concentration on economics in the fourth year (it forms a topic for all the language teaching for an entire term) no training in specialist areas is offered, except in as much as students at any Scottish university are able to take optional courses – so called 'electives' – during the first two years of their studies. (Some do, indeed, take specialist courses, such as computer studies, although others use the opportunity to take up a third language.) A traditional concern in Scottish education has been to retain a breadth of education at secondary and tertiary level. It is reflected in the examination system at secondary level and, at tertiary level, perhaps offers a model which universities elsewhere in Great Britain could emulate. Unfortunately the financial constraints under which universities are operating seem to be leading to a gradual crumbling of this excellent system.

One question included in my questionnaire to industry was the extent to which firms felt that the linguists they recruited had deficiencies in specialist knowledge. The majority of those who replied stated that their recruits usually did not have any knowledge of the specialist area they were to work in, but that they regarded that as the firm's task to rectify. And many of them detailed the measures they took to familiarise their linguists with their products or processes. This was to be expected. Given that there are still very few subject specialists who convert into translators at an early age, firms recruiting younger staff inevitably have to recruit people who are 'mere' linguists. We have already heard from John Graham and Doug Embleton details of the excellent training schemes operated by ICI and Mannesmann.

One or two of the firms who replied did, however, state that what was important was that recruits should have had some experience of tackling any highly specialised area – in other words they should know how to go about problem-solving, reading their way into a subject, tackling the question of terminology. The procedural skills involved are transferable. This is, of course, an area of training where the post-graduate courses offer excellent preparation, by their use of subject specialists as lecturers. But it is also feasible at undergraduate level – as can be demonstrated from the example of the German translator/interpreter training institutions.

Practical skills

Though what I have termed procedural skills can be taught at university, subject knowledge I would therefore see as belonging largely to the sphere of knowledge and skills which it is more appropriate for young translators to acquire after their basic training at university. This sphere includes also what have been termed practical skills – office skills such as typing, dictating, word processing. In addition to a faculty pool, Heriot-Watt has 15 IBM-compatible word processors and 4 printers to which students in the department have exclusive and open access. Apart from one optional introductory session word processing is, however, not formally taught, neither is any instruction in basic typing or other office skills offered. The majority of students do familiarise themselves with word processing during the four years of the course. Strong motivation is provided by the two dissertations which they have to write at the end of their year abroad – and present in typed and bound form. The cost of getting these typed professionally is usually an incentive for learning to type oneself.

Among the replies received from the questionnaire to industry the majority of firms played down the importance of word processing skills. The questionnaire did not enquire into the extent to which word processing was actually carried out by the translators involved. Some employers, however, made it clear that they taught such skills to their recruits. Others possibly did not require such skills at all. It may be that in this respect – and in the case of specialist subjects – the trainers worry too much about teaching specific skills to students. What would seem to be more important is a very thorough grounding in basic linguistic skills, including coping with terminology problems.

Where should these skills be acquired?

If one returns to my original list of components involved in translator training, it would seem that the first two components, mother tongue competence and foreign-language competence, can be assigned to the domain of the universities and polytechnics (although more thought needs to be devoted to the development of strategies for improving the former, and provision for continuous improvement of both areas should be provided throughout a linguist's career). The acquisition of specific subject knowledge and practical skills should occur as in-service training, involving firms, training institutions and the ITI. This should not, however, be taken to mean acceptance of the suggestion that the universities and polytechnics should concentrate on language acquisition alone – general translation competence, as I have attempted to demonstrate, is something which can also be acquired as an undergraduate, though obviously an increase in translation competence is also something which occurs on the job as well. This area therefore would be another where pre-job and in-service training complement each other.

CONCLUSION

I would like finally to return to the four points from Michael Croft's paper which I singled out at the start. Points 1 and 4 I have already largely dealt with. As far as point 2 is concerned, I would suggest that in the British context while it is utterly appropriate for the translation element in undergraduate courses to be taught by experienced and practising translators – and they would therefore be involved also in assessment procedures – it would not be appropriate to involve the profession in any formal way in controlling the examination process. This would, as Michael Croft pointed out, have far-reaching implications in terms of failure rates, and would represent a radical and to my mind unnecessary reorientation of the role of undergraduate courses in the British education system. Professional examinations should come at a later stage. I see a very important role for bodies such as the ITI – possibly in conjunction with the training institutions – in providing a later qualification for full entry into the profession, a goal to be worked towards by young recruits in much the same way as occurs in professions such as accountancy or banking.

A scheme such as this would partly solve the third problem posed by Michael Croft: the extent to which training courses should respond to the perceived needs of the market. It is notoriously difficult to adapt what goes on in a four-year university course to the immediate and changing needs of the market. While long term trends, such as the increasing importance of Japanese or the resurgence of demand for Russian can be reacted to, short-term demand is something which the ITI, the suppliers of short courses and industry itself are in a better position to respond to.

RECOMMENDATIONS

There have been two strands running through this paper: firstly an awareness of the particular traditions of our education system, the pressures to which it is being exposed and the constraints within which it operates; secondly the need for some sort of global view of what is appropriate for translator training and what balance should be struck between institutional training and in-service training. The two strands need to be drawn together. I would suggest that a fundamental review of what we require of translator training similar to that carried out by the BDÜ is called for. However, to avoid this resulting in a theoretical model which cannot then be put into practice, those responsible should keep in mind the realities of the educational scene in Britain in the 1990s. These realities will probably mean that if there is to be a significant expansion in the numbers of young translators to meet the challenges posed by the completion of the Single Market, then this will have to be done initially mainly at undergraduate level. We should not be unduly dismayed by this prospect. I have argued in this paper that satisfactory training can be carried out at undergraduate level. In an ideal world, this basic training would be deepened and intensified at postgraduate level. However, this may be demanding too much. Moreover, as Michael Croft indicated last year, the future of funding for post-graduate courses in Britain hangs in the balance. It is desirable that these should at least continue to supply the sort of conversion courses for linguists which they offer at present. Problems of funding may, however, mean that they will need to shift the emphasis and develop further the modular courses which some of them already run. These would then be attended by linguists already in employment and funded by their firms, perhaps on the basis of being released for training one day per week. Furthermore, there would seem to be a role for training institutes in supplying short courses in specialised areas for practising linguists at all levels of experience. (This was mentioned by a number of those replying to my questionnaire – and there are, indeed, already some notable examples of such courses being run by, for example, Bradford, Salford and PCL.) These would cover not just special subjects such as law or statistics but also training in further languages of which the linguist requires knowledge, and as such would complement the product-specific training given wholly within firms. A prerequisite for all such courses would be recognition by industry of the importance of continuing training for their linguists and a willingness to back this recognition with financial support.

It should be emphasised once again that an institution such as the ITI can play a central role in co-ordinating and advising on the implementation of the above ideas.

REFERENCES

[1] CROFT, M. '21 years of the postgraduate course in Bath'. In Picken, C. (ed.) *ITI Conference 2: Translators and Interpreters mean Business*, London: Aslib, 1988.
[2] BDÜ Memorandum 'Praxis und Lehre'. *Mitteilungsblatt für Dolmetscher und Übersetzer*, 5/32 pp 2–8.
[3] *Languages at Heriot-Watt University, Edinburgh.* Leaflet available from this paper's author.
[4] REISS, K. *Texttyp und Übersetzungsmethode; der operative Text*, Kronberg, 1976.

Continuing education for translating and interpreting

Karin R.M. Band

Freelance translator and conference interpreter

If the licence to practise meant the completion of his education how sad it would be for the practitioner, how distressing to his patients! More clearly than any other the physician should illustrate the truth of Plato's saying that education is a life-long process.   William Osler, 1900[1]

INTRODUCTION

It may seem slightly preposterous to start a lecture on continuing education for linguists by quoting a text written for doctors. However, it should not be too difficult to translate the quotation to our profession; there is not much in the literature of our profession that could be used as a quote; and as a profession that has not as yet set itself any formal training requirements (or, indeed, any training requirements at all), we could do worse than study what has been done by a profession that has a formal training system (and thus a benchmark for continuing education); that has made continuing education a duty for its members; and that has evolved and implemented such concepts as credit hours, peer review, periodic re-examination, and, indeed, relicensure.[2]

TERMINOLOGY AND SCOPE

Different authors use different terms. Thus one finds 'continuing' as well as 'postgraduate', 'education' as well as 'training'. I have decided to use 'continuing', to reflect the life-long commitment mentioned by Plato; to take into account that not all linguists have a degree; and to avoid confusion with the term 'postgraduate' as applied to various courses that serve as a preparation for entry into the profession (and are therefore, strictly speaking, graduate, if not undergraduate training). Also, I have opted for 'education' rather than 'training', since, at the level considered here, 'the term "training" should be avoided as it implies a master/pupil relation-ship inappropriate to fully qualified (practitioners)';[3] and because education is concerned with higher goals than the mere transmission of knowledge and skills. Thus, in this lecture, we will be looking at continuing education (CE), which could be defined as educational activities for established practitioners. The emphasis will be on the needs of the generalist, since even those linguists who wish to specialise would have to maintain a considerable breadth of education; this lecture will not concern itself with job-specific research (in preparation for a particular translation or conference), nor with training schemes provided by industrial or other organisations.

CONTENT

Although the educational problem may be greater for linguists than for members of other professions, in that we require not only factual knowledge but also the ability to express this knowledge in different languages, our profession still lacks a formal training system and agreed standards, which makes it difficult to define the content of CE for linguists.

The basic needs to be met have been described[3] as:

- filling up gaps in knowledge, skills and attitudes
- refreshing and renewing previously obtained knowledge and skills
- obtaining new specific knowledge and skills
- keeping up to date with new developments.

I have called these requirements 'top up' and 'keep up', for short.

TOP-UP

This is the need, at the start of a linguist's working life, to fill in any gaps in knowledge (where 'knowledge' means both factual and linguistic knowledge, and where 'linguistic' also includes the linguist's mother tongue) and skills. It is at this level that the greatest diversity exists, since what the novice knows or does not know will be a function of his or her previous education and experience, including such factors as family background, age, nationality and formal educational history; and unlike other professions, ours has a great many portals of entry. It is obvious that the baseline level and pattern of knowledge will be different depending on whether training has been in the form of a four-year course or a two-term course; or whether an expert in a certain field has decided to use his or her knowledge of a language or languages to work as a linguist. However, it should also be remembered that even a broad-based, systematic four-year course will leave its graduates with a need for top-up – although, as we shall see below, having been on, or at least knowing the content of, such a course, can be very useful in directing the practising linguist's CE efforts.

KEEP-UP

This term refers to the requirements that arise after the linguist has embarked on a career. Here, the need is much more uniform, and should, indeed, be the same for any one 'crop' of linguists starting out at the same time. Like top-up, keep-up is concerned both with factual knowledge and with linguistic knowledge (including, once again, each linguist's mother tongue). Whilst the progress of technology (and hence the need for updating one's factual knowledge) is obvious even to the person in the street, linguists themselves sometimes seem to overlook the way in which language evolves. And yet, through extrinsic and intrinsic pressures, language – in all its aspects and at all levels – is changing all the time. Thus the challenge to linguists is to top up the knowledge they have at the start of their career, and to keep up with developments thereafter. Which brings us to the question of how to meet these requirements.

INDIVIDUAL VERSUS ORGANISED CE

It has been said at times that, whereas all the other professions are furthering CE for their members, linguists are not doing anything. However, things may not be as uniformly bad as this statement seems to imply. (To take the example of a very mundane – and very necessary – activity: reading a daily newspaper, or at least a weekly news magazine, in one's language of habitual use and one's other languages. Perhaps because it is so mundane, it is not properly considered as the CE instrument it is. And yet the daily/weekly press is a powerful source of top-up, and even more so of keep-up, providing an update on the way in which the world around us and the language(s) evolve.) In medicine, too, it is recognised that CE has two components: individual CE and organised CE. [3] The difference between the two professions resides in the balance between the two components.

Individual CE

As things stand nowadays, linguists need to rely much more heavily than doctors on individual efforts to meet their CE needs. The organised side is still less well developed, although there is now a growing awareness of the need for a more formal approach, and solutions are being evolved. However, the very different knowledge and skill backgrounds at entry, and, to some extent, the different aspects of the work of practising linguists, mean that individual CE will remain the priority requirement. This is why a linguist must be a 'self-starter' – the sort of person that can use what Edward de Bono has termed 'lateral thinking' [4] to decide what they need or might need, and how to get it. Basically, there are two categories of acquisition: knowledge acquisition, and resource acquisition. The daily/weekly press has already been mentioned as a source of knowledge. Other free or inexpensive sources would be television, local libraries, popular science publications, museums, etc. The term 'resources' covers both the 'hardware' of word processors, typewriters and dictaphones, and the 'software' – encyclopaedias, dictionaries, reference books and subscriptions to general or specific press products. Apart from the actual acquisition of resources, there is also the aspect of *resource research*. This is not a fancy term for such things as visits to the more specialist bookshops to see what is on offer; finding out about reference libraries and their conditions of access; setting up a network of people that could provide expert advice as and when required: I am using the term deliberately to show that this activity is part of CE (and therefore, like all CE efforts, tax deductible). It is also important to remember that this research should be conducted both at home and, whenever possible, abroad – as part, perhaps, of the one vital requirement for all linguists' CE, the stay abroad at regular intervals in the country (or countries) in which their language(s) is (are) spoken. It goes without saying that these trips, too, are (or should be) tax deductible, as part of CE.

One aspect that should not be overlooked is that of *non-linguistic work-related subjects* – such things as the 3 Rs as they apply to our profession (e.g. rapid reading; speedwriting, consecutive note-taking; tax and VAT); legal and ethical questions; voice training; and – to use lateral thinking – even body language.

Organised CE

Whilst many of the above subjects have been pursued by individual linguists, the organised side of CE is still patchy and inconsistent. Compared with the medical profession, we are at a disadvantage by not having a supplying industry that sponsors lectures and courses (albeit as part of a marketing exercise), or a monolithic client such as the NHS that can allow paid CE leave. (Even in the single-client relationship enjoyed by staff translators/interpreters, not enough allowance seems to be made for paid CE leave.) However, with a growing awareness of the profession's ethical duty to engage in CE, certain activities (and indeed patterns⋆) are emerging. ITI itself organises workshops and runs networks, and publishes a calendar of activities, of which many are CE-related. Schools in different parts of the world have risen to the demand by organising events such as the English Update Course first run by the Polytechnic of Central London three years ago (and since then repeated here and 'exported' to other countries), or the refresher course on consecutive interpreting run by Geneva University. Private initiatives have led to such schemes as the Medical Translators Workshops (one-day events held several times a year). There is also increased interest in what can be provided by cultural institutes, or by higher education institutions (for those linguists who wish to pursue specialisation to degree level).

The good news, then, is that much of what is needed is being catered for. However, there are problems, both for the organiser and the participant. For the organiser, the problem consists in the heterogeneity of the target group (different interests, different levels, often different countries). It may be difficult to find the right time or the right location. For the would-be participant, there are the usual problems of time and money, but also – and most critically, perhaps – of lack of information.

WHAT WE NEED

The first requirement, therefore, is that of an information centre, a focus that would provide the following functions:

- to pool and disseminate information on courses, lectures, and other CE-related events, along the lines of the list now being drawn up by ITI;
- to act as a link between previous and potential organisers, to advise on patterns and pitfalls;
- to survey and report demand (indeed, to create demand, by showing linguists what subjects they could study, especially under the heading of top-up. For this purpose, it would be useful to have a specimen syllabus, which could be derived from such sources as the BDÜ paper, the actual contents of broad-based long-term courses (at different universities), and suggestions from the field. The idea would be to have a checklist against which linguists could decide what to go for in their individual CE efforts, or what sort of courses to suggest to potential organisers.)

This kind of focus could well be provided by the professional institutes. Similarly, the institutes and the schools would have a role to play in the provision of classes or courses to respond to the demand perceived (or created). Also, the senior colleagues should be aware of their responsibility for the next generation of linguists. Wherever possible, experienced practitioners should do some of the teaching in order to pass on their expertise and skill.

However, there is one point that should be borne in mind in all organised CE activities, whether these activities are provided by professional institutes, by the schools, or by individual colleagues: what the profession needs is not only learning facilities and a focus for information, but a *locus* – a physical place where colleagues can meet. Without this social forum those who usually work by themselves will be deprived of peer contact. And without peer contact, we, as a profession, will not be able to go on to the peer review and peer audit principles already established in other professions.

CONCLUSION

The main point to remember is this: as a profession, we may not as yet have a formal training system that would provide a common baseline against which the requirement for CE can be gauged. However, that deficiency does not absolve us from the ethical duty of undertaking CE. In fact, this duty is more than just a vaguely moral one. For the established practitioner, CE is the only way to *quality assurance*.

$$CE = QA$$

And in an age of increasingly 'defensive' practice, and product liability, CE is a legal duty – a duty of common sense. The word duty usually implies a burden – and CE, whether individual or organised, does require an effort, and expenditure of time, money and energy. However, we should perhaps try to see it more as a privilege than a burden. CE is a way of asking what we can do for the profession, to assure its quality and thereby improve its standing. The profession itself is generous enough: with everything we do, and the research undertaken in support of our work, we are allowed to learn, to broaden our horizon. Or, as a colleague once put it, 'we get paid life-long for educating ourselves'.

REFERENCES

[1] OSLER, W. In [2]
[2] RICHARDS, R.K. *Continuing medical education*: perspectives, problems, prognosis, Yale University Press, 1978.
[3] MEISCH, G. 'Continuing education in medicine: II', in: *Medical education and manpower in the EEC*. Ed. Sir John Walton and T.B. Binns. Milan: Fondazione Smith Kline, 1984.
[4] DE BONO, E. *Lateral thinking*, London: Pelican Books, 1977.

* One pattern that has proved useful in different settings (English Update, Medical Translators Workshops, Course of Medical English for Translators and Interpreters) is the EFTA – Expert First, Translations Afterwards – i.e. a lecture given by an expert in the field, to provide an introduction to, and sometimes help with, the text(s) to be translated by the group.

Session 3: Report of discussion

Rapporteur: Melanie Dean, Rhône-Poulenc Ltd

Jane Taylor, as chairman, thanked both Karin Band and Hugh Keith for their valuable contributions and invited questions and comments from the audience.

Commenting on Hugh Keith's paper, 'University versus in-service training', John Graham, Mannesmann Demag, felt that too many people opted to study translation and interpreting without having more than a layperson's conception of what exactly was involved. He said that he knew of no adequate method of assessing the aptitude of the student for this profession. He wondered whether, in fact, universities and polytechnics were teaching the right people in the wrong manner or vice-versa. At Duisburg University, students now studied translation as part of the MA course in Anglistik. In view of this, John Graham felt that students should be taught how to acquire translation skills at this level. Addressing his final comment to Karin Band, he said that a former President of the Swiss Translation Association once very neatly described the freelance translator/interpreter as a *'spécialiste généraliste'*.

In reply, Hugh Keith agreed that, despite studying a four-year course in translation and interpreting, a number of students clearly were not destined to enter the profession. He went on to explain that at Heriot-Watt University candidates for the translation and interpreting course were subjected to a very rigorous interview designed to assess motivation and mother-tongue competence.

Pamela Mayorcas, freelance, London, expressed her concern as regards training translators/interpreters at undergraduate level. She wondered whether there were economic and political pressures forcing universities and polytechnics to train language specialists at this level. Surely competent translation and interpreting could only be carried out by practitioners with a degree, a postgraduate conversion course supplemented by work experience and continuing training?

Hugh Keith explained that higher education establishments had, in fact, been forced into a situation where translation and interpreting had to be taught at under-graduate level. Companies should supplement this by providing further training for their linguists, particularly as regards acquisition of subject knowledge and practical skills.

Commenting on the applied language courses available in the UK, Gordon Stuart, freelance, Scotland, enquired whether Hugh Keith would agree that in order to assist with the training of translators and interpreters some of the more traditional universities should offer courses with less of a literary bias.

In response, Hugh Keith said that many universities and polytechnics were now trying to adapt their courses to meet market trends. This, he felt, was to be discouraged since the applied courses such as those available at Heriot-Watt, Salford, Bradford and Bath universities were very specific and only suitably qualified staff should be recruited to teach these skills.

Referring to the theme of Karin Band's paper, continuing education for translating and interpreting, Claude Fleurent, Rhône-Poulenc Ltd, Essex, asked whether any progress had been made in the past year as regards the availability of postgraduate modular courses in the Home Counties.

Jane Taylor, University of Manchester, replied that the ITI's Training and Education Committee was doing its best to encourage universities and polytechnics to introduce such courses but the problem of funding remained the major obstacle.

In response to the question of aptitude tests, Paul Perkins, freelance, Gateshead, suggested that in order to ensure that only the most suitable students were accepted on to an applied languages course, candidates should take an aptitude test, the pass mark for which should be set at, say, 60 per cent. Anyone failing to achieve this should not be allowed on to the course.

Hugh Keith explained that educational institutions had considered a procedure along these lines, whereby only the most gifted students would be accepted on to the course. However, not all universities and polytechnics could afford to be so selective. Unfortunately, as is nearly always the case these days, it is a matter of funds.

Session 4: Legal and ethical issues

Chaired by Roger Fletcher

The speakers at this session, Kate Pool (Translators Association), Robert Clark (freelance) and Hilde Watson (freelance) gave brief informal presentations – not reported – followed by a discussion.

Session 4: Report of discussion

Rapporteur: Martin Lovell-Pank

Gordon Stuart (freelance) asked what was the cost of professional indemnity for freelances. E. Seaton (freelance) mentioned that years ago a broker offered the Institute of Linguists preferential rates. Members of the audience gave varying figures: £450 per annum for £250,000, £175 for £50,000, £250 for £100,000. (In France it seems to be cheaper than in England: £100 for £100,000.) It was remarked that the premium also depended on turnover and deductible amounts.

John Graham (freelance, Germany) said he only knew of about three cases in 25 years of professionals being sued in Germany. He mentioned restrictions on working at home, which exist because, for example, a translator's assets could be compromised if he was sued in the event of the consequences of a mistake. The claim would take precedence over the rights of the building society. Hilde Watson (freelance) said she understood her flat could not be taken away from her. Roger Fletcher commented that the higher the insurance, the higher the claim. Robert Clark (translator) suggested that as most of us were sole traders, we would not be liable like a limited company. Sue Marshall (Bank of England) suggested that the very low number of translators sued might be due to the fact that John Graham was taking Germany as an example.

Nicholas Chadwick (freelance) asked what the effect would be of expressly disclaiming product liability. Peter Barber (Able Translations) stated that it could be argued whether this constituted fair trading, as you had to be confident to do a job. A freelance translator remarked that the deeds of her house forbid her to establish a public house or a boarding house (which she had no intention of setting up!) but that local authorities worried more about noise or similar nuisance. Graham Cross (freelance) pointed out that professional indemnity is issued for the year the claim is made, not when the negligence is alleged, so it must be taken out permanently. And as regards the use of the home for business, there are rights according to which an Englishman may apply his craft in his own home if he does not commit nuisance.

K. Band (freelance) said that we must bear in mind the references and background reading on which our translations are based. With reference to Hilde Watson's problem, she suggested that all interpreting be taped and the interpreter could decide on the use of the tape. We were now entering a more 'defensive' age. References to dictionaries no longer stood up, and even dictionaries issued disclaimers. Hilde Watson was advised to take out legal expense insurance, a concept apparently introduced from Germany.

Peter Barber said response from ITI members on professional indemnity insurance had been very poor, (less than 30 comments on the proposed scheme), and no insurance broker would be prepared to organise a scheme on such a small scale. Robert Clark (speaker) mentioned the Federation of Self-Employed and Small Businesses, who have several insurance schemes, including one covering investigation by the Inland Revenue! Roger Fletcher said that premiums could be negotiated. He had been approached for a higher premium but got it substantially reduced.

Dr R.G. Hooper (freelance, Germany), worked in Germany and inquired about the copyright position for staff translators. Kate Pool said copyright belongs normally to the employer but if work was done for a publisher, the translator's name must appear.

Next, Pamela Mayorcas described a recent occasion on which she had been given an assignment for translation. She suspected it had already been translated and indeed found the translation in Brussels. The agency told her to send the original direct to the client. What would her colleagues have done? Claude Fleurent (translator), advised her to charge for her time. Cate Avery (translator) said that some clients ask for a back translation to check accuracy.

Peter Arthern (translator) said he had sometimes been instructed to translate in a certain way which was inaccurate, and asked what his colleagues would have done. Peter Barber advised refusing it. There was wide agreement with this. Robert Dewsnap (freelance, Sweden), asked if the ITI had some machinery to deal with problems of this kind. Lanna Castellano said there was an arbitration committee and a procedure. She mentioned that the same translation is often asked for twice. If you said you had already done it for somebody else, it would be a breach of confidence. Also, would it be a breach of copyright? Peter Barber thought the client should pay for it, as there was no obligation to keep material on file. It was accepted practice that a translator sells the copyright as part of the translation fee. This means you had no right to the copy kept on file. Perhaps you could improve on it! Roger Fletcher remarked that if you had to do any work involving either reading or making corrections or similar, you should invoice the client.

Karin Band (translator) said what if one were asked to translate in a manner one disagreed with. Some things might conflict with customs or practice in another country. Her method was to put a note in the translation stating her position. Claude Fleurent commented that all you could do would be to draw attention to something, and that this depended on the relationship with the client. He would always warn his own firm about something.

Cate Avery (staff translator) brought up the question of the percentage charged by agencies. The translation company could not charge a flat percentage to its client as this would mean a wide disparity in its rates. Gordon Stuart (freelance) said it was accepted that an agency took 33⅓ per cent Martin Lovell-Pank (freelance) said he had ascertained that there was very great disparity in the fees charged by agencies, exceeding 100 per cent. Graham Cross (freelance) agreed and said he had found a 100 per cent difference too between the percentage charged by the agencies but remarked that he had also found a 100 per cent difference between the fees charged by freelance translators. An agency representative remarked that it should be taken into account that agencies had to correct and revise freelance translations and that this entailed varying amounts of work.

Chris Percival referred to Hilde Watson's being sued and said he would like to hear about experiences from people who had had to take others to court. He had taken legal action in three countries, the UK, France and Germany. In the UK he found a successful County Court action practically useless. In Germany he won the case but would not sue again. In France he decided to have the client pestered instead of bringing legal action. Tristam Carrington-Windo (freelance) took a client to court in Germany but remarked that a good lawyer was essential. Roger Fletcher asked how many would sue for payment (show of hands: a third of the audience would sue); and how many of those who work abroad (show of hands: about half would sue).

Florence Mitchell (freelance) asked if anybody had experience of debt collectors. A freelance translator in the audience recommended them, so as to avoid legal nuisance for oneself. She said the firms were very efficient. Paul Knighton (freelance) believed one should pursue a claim. Eyvor Fogarty (freelance) said that if the Small Claims Court was involved (under £500), you did not have to sue. She also reminded the audience that ITI had got people to pay simply by saying that otherwise no translator would work for them again. Paul Knighton said that that worked with agencies but not with direct clients. John Griffin (freelance) said that the non-payers must be pestered and he even asked one client for advance payment. John Graham recalled that he gave a translator an assignment for a trade fair and that the work was delivered three months late. Susana Greiss, freelance, mentioned that in America there is a Small Claims Court. She threatened to take a law firm to court but they settled because lawyers hate to be taken to court. Also the New York chapter of the American Translators Association has a 'sick list' of customers with bad reputations. ATA members were asked to put their problems in writing. Roger Fletcher mentioned that we had to be careful in the UK because of the libel laws. Paul Knighton (translator) said that clients should be pursued and not be allowed to get away with malpractice. Mansour Awad (French court interpreter) remarked that they sometimes had problems in being paid and that he received clients in his office to ascertain where they came from, because they had his address but he did not have theirs.

The chairman then read out a message from the FIT congratulating the ITI.

Session 5: Translation forum

Chaired by Peter Barber

Auto-didacticism as a way of life

Ben Teague

Self-employed translator, Athens, Georgia, USA

At home I keep a file labelled 'WTBAT' for 'Wants To Be A Translator'. When students and displaced professionals call seeking translation work, I talk with them and carefully record their names and abilities; then after a month I throw away the notes. I do not seem to lose much of value, for along with their precious and unique virtues these people have one common lack: awareness of what I regard as a central skill of translating, the ability to become a specialist.

I earned a university degree in physics, yet the literature of physics has accounted for only a tiny part of my 17 years' translation work. Early in my career I translated chiefly Russian journal articles on oilfield hardware and chemical engineering; later I acquired clients with interests in materials science and nuclear engineering; like most of my colleagues, I have never quite managed to fend off computer software jobs. And for nearly four years I have been much occupied with books on the theory and practice of geodesy.

Two factors have shaped my work profile: market demand and my own skills and inclinations. Most physics translation from Russian takes place in two vast cover-to-cover operations, of which one seeks working physicists only while the other pays low rates and expects the poor work that actually does result. By comparison, materials science – metallurgy, strength of materials, testing, etc. – is a diffuse field. Researchers find some of their data in product brochures and other 'non-literary' sources. Even the articles and books they wish to read are not in great enough demand to have spurred the kind of blanket translation effort seen in physics. Strong demand therefore exists for 'custom' translation services.

What is more, being able to 'learn' new areas of knowledge is a marketable skill in itself. My nuclear engineer clients find my services more valuable because I can adapt to changes in their interests (from metallurgical analysis of fission-reactor vessels to inertial fusion, to take one instance).

Recently, since undertaking to translate works on geodesy, I have had occasion to think about this process of acquiring new fields. (Geodesy is the science that studies the Earth's shape and gravitational field along with methods of determining the positions and directions of points and lines on its surface. I mention this because, at the time of undertaking the project, I could not have confidently defined the word myself.) In this talk I want to pose questions that translators must ask when facing a similar opportunity and, more hesitantly, suggest some answers as well.

CAN I LEARN ENOUGH ABOUT THIS UNFAMILIAR TOPIC?

A more immediate and disturbing question might be: why is the topic unfamiliar? If it is related in some close way to a field that one already knows, the extension may be a simple matter of paging through the chapters never read in an old textbook. But if the new area is a mystery and so are all the allied fields, one must step carefully.

The worst case is that one does not know much about the field (perhaps cannot even define it), does not know much about allied subjects, and does not have access to text and reference books about it. The best involves building on a good knowledge of, say, sedimentary geology to cover petroleum geology. Nearly every real-world case falls between, and how the translator finally answers the question will depend not only on resources and prior knowledge but also on experience. My experience tells me, for example, that I can quickly get oriented in organic chemistry or the measurement of visual-field defects, but not in the chemistry of vision.

Although this is the first question in my series, it is commonly the hardest as well.

WILL IT PAY TO LEARN IT?

Translators always take account of economics in deciding whether and how to acquire new expertise. Consider an article and a translator who could produce a high-quality translation in 24 working hours if the topic were a familiar one. The rates are such that the translator gets a reasonable fee for the 24 hours' work. But *this* job will require 48 hours of preparation along with the 24 hours for translation. After a short-term analysis, the translator will very likely turn down the assignment, and properly.

There are other considerations, though. First, the job may lead to a long, life-giving series of jobs. (This is not the same as to say the client promises a long series of jobs. Clients always do that.) The analysis changes: the 48 hours' (or two months') study can then be set off against a dozen or a hundred assignments, so that the proposition may turn out to be a profitable one. Second, the translator may judge that this client is worth the investment (an otherwise useful relationship might not survive a refusal) and may decide to 'eat' the 48 hours' fee. Third, a client who has sent out a hundred chemistry articles and now has one product bulletin on paint may not need the same expert-quality work that was required on the chemical jobs; in short, it may be all right to study paint for 4 hours instead of 48.

My experience provides me with a rule of thumb: for an established client, do the research unless it relates to the life sciences or the social 'sciences'. For a new (cold) contact, offer to help find the right translator for the job. In one case, I even extended the rule to cover a new language: a senior client sent a short Bulgarian article, thinking it was in Russian; it dealt with a familiar topic; the client was receptive to a higher rate if it would save the trouble of finding another translator. I did the research (studied Bulgarian for a time I do not care to specify) and met my client's need.

BUT MY RESOURCES ARE LIMITED. HOW CAN I PUT THEM TO BEST USE?

Translators always work under constraints of one kind or another. The pinch is worst when it comes to money and time. Indeed, whether the new field is accessible at all depends on what resources the translator can gather and exploit in the time available. My experience with geodesy leads me to a few suggestions:

Obtain a quick, rough orientation before doing anything else. Read an encyclopaedia article, for example, and take a few notes. At this point it should be clear where the new field stands in relation to ones that are already familiar; the notes should contain some key terms and ideas; and even this short course of reading may yield a small bibliography. The most cursory search on geodesy will identify some important concepts (ellipsoid of revolution versus triaxial ellipsoid, gravity versus gravitation) and important names (Heiskanen, Molodensky).

Begin the translation right after the orientation reading. The introduction to a book or the abstract of an article will at least suggest what general topics will and will not be taken up. My first large assignment in geodesy started out by establishing that the author's concerns lay in geodetic networks (sets of points and lines on the ground that form the basis or 'control' for national and local surveys), but also incidentally by stating that satellites, geodetic instruments and the large-scale shape of the Earth would not be major topics. Knowing this enabled me to edit my list of needed references.

After translating a few hundred or a few thousand words, take stock. Are the references on the list the correct ones? Get hold of some primary target-language materials and read or scan them, noting both terminology (with definitions) and relationships. My file on one geodesy translation includes not only the terms 'Laplace's surface spherical harmonics' and 'Legendre functions' but also the note, 'Surface spherical harmonics are Legendre functions multiplied by $\cos m\lambda$ or $\sin m\lambda$.'

Keep notes of problems encountered in the text and how they were solved. Another of my files says, '*Mezhdunarodnoye byuro vremeni* = *Bureau International de l'Heure?* Yes – client confirms.'

Once resolved to learn a new field, spend reasonable amounts on resources. A copy of Bomford's *Geodesy*[1] or Heiskanen and Moritz's *Physical Geodesy*[2] in the office is worth two in the university library.

At some point well into the translation, declare a research day. Organise a list of questions and a thermos of coffee and head for the library. Work through all available texts, ask librarians for help, even cast about at random. On a recent job I delayed until the first draft was complete, then spent two days reading. Some answers came not from books on geodesy but from those on practical astronomy.

Keep careful notes of preferred terms, changes, useful sources and so forth, and have them available for future use.

Adopt a system of terminology storage and retrieval. A shoebox of index cards is better than a notebook, and a database program (I favour Mercury/Termex, which is specifically designed for use by translators) is better than a shoebox.

HOW CAN I EVALUATE WHAT I HAVE DONE?

If the hardest question to answer was 'Can I learn this?' then the hardest part of the programme is assessing the results. The translator starts out as a person with, by hypothesis, no knowledge in the new field and, by implication, no judgment either. There are, however, some expedients that make an evaluation possible.

Remember that there are two kinds of translations: those that are perfect and those that are done. In particular, the ability to translate a geodetic document does not imply the ability to write an original one.

Keep in mind that the client probably knows more about the topic than he or she has let on. Asking intelligent questions will make a better impression than submitting a translation that is full of footnotes or, worse yet, bad terminology. The most intelligent question of all is, 'Which publications *of yours* might I consult for help on this project?'

Learn the art of protective coloration. When producing a text on geodesy, try to write as geodesists do. If a source-language sentence does not easily translate into a proper sentence in the language of geodesy, there is a good chance the translator has not understood it yet.

Examine all work for internal consistency. If the translation says, 'No theory has been developed. A comprehensive theoretical treatment of this topic appears in Heiskanen and Moritz', one sentence or the other may be wrong.

Use target-language references as a check. A translated sentence that contradicts Bomford's text may be right (the author may have advanced knowledge beyond what Bomford knew), but it should attract the translator's severest inspection.

A great Tennessean said, 'Be sure you're right; then go ahead'. A proofreader's maxim says, 'Follow copy out the window'. Allow the author the dignity of being wrong, once it is certain the translation does not just make him or her *seem* to be wrong. (And spare the reader any hint of sarcasm in the footnotes.)

Cultivate a specialist, whether for casual help with terminology or for subcontract work as reviser.

Badger the client for evaluations and suggestions, not from the librarian or purchasing department but from the specialists who will use the work.

Learning a new speciality is often a realistic programme, and no translator should shy from the attempt on principle. But any such effort requires great care, self-awareness and a substantial amount of time. Since every translator strives to make quality measure up to fees and vice versa, even the ability to assess a new field and plan an approach to it is of value. My four questions:

- Can I do it?
- Will it pay?

- How can I put my resources to best use?
- How good is this work?

represent one paradigm for the needed analysis.

REFERENCES

[1]   BOMFORD, G. *Geodesy*, 4th Ed. Oxford University Press, 1980. (An admirable compendium of theory and practice; not, unfortunately, a reliable source of terminology, since the author uses his own words for some techniques and describes others without naming them.)

[2]   HEISKANEN, W.A. and MORITZ, H. *Physical geodesy*. Freeman, 1967. (Standard treatment of physical and mathematical aspects of the Earth's gravitational field.)

The glasnost explosion: monitoring Soviet broadcasts in a time of change

Mike Hollow

BBC Monitoring

One way of gauging the cultural impact a country has made on the world is to look at the number and the nature of its words which have acquired an international currency. Five years ago, if such a question had been put to the average Westerner concerning the Russian language, the chances are they would have come up with *Bolshevik* and *sputnik* and not much more. It is not surprising, therefore, that to many citizens of today's USSR it is a matter of some pride that the words which have become the twin slogans of their new revolution – *glasnost* and *perestroyka* – have also become familiar to the eyes and ears of the whole world.

Amongst the first of those eyes and ears outside the USSR were, of course, the linguists employed at BBC Monitoring. For 50 years now the BBC has been monitoring the world's public broadcasting services, listening to their news as they report it and turning it rapidly – at times immediately – into our news through the application of fast and accurate translation skills. Nowadays BBC Monitoring employs over 120 linguists working in some 30 languages at its headquarters in Caversham, Berkshire. For those engaged in monitoring Soviet radio and television broadcasts the Gorbachev years have brought a number of new linguistic challenges. Even the appearance of the word *glasnost* itself posed a problem. For us, leaving a new term untranslated is the last resort, but even the best anyone could do with *glasnost* – 'openness' – failed to convey the full flavour of the word and proved inadequate when *glasnost* was juxtaposed with the normal word for 'openness' *otkrytost*. So *glasnost* it has remained.

The work of monitoring is an unusual cross between interpreting and translating. We have to produce a full and accurate translation on paper, but our source material is what we hear rather than what we can see. Moreover we are separated from the speaker we are translating by thousands of miles: a problem often compounded by poor radio reception conditions. The linguist, or monitor, has to acquire the skill of hearing accurately through all the impediments of reception, acoustics and diction, and must have a wide vocabulary: looking up a word you have never heard before is not easy when you cannot see it! The monitor must also be linguistically capable of dealing with any subject which may crop up in a day's radio or TV broadcasting.

The advent of Mr Gorbachev has turned the Soviet media upside down. The broadcasting media have been in the forefront of pushing back the boundaries of discussion, and the formerly taboo subjects, whether it be drug abuse, prostitution or life in Stalin's labour camps, have one by one been brought under the spotlight. New and snappier programme formats have been introduced, with studio discussions, vox pop interviews and off-the-cuff chat by presenters. The difficulties of understanding and translating the mumbled comments of a Soviet punk rocker on any subject are considerable, and the problem is worse when the interview is a recording of inferior quality made on the street.

Not that the problem is any easier with the country's leader. Mr Gorbachev has two characteristics which make life difficult for us: one is that he likes to talk a lot to all sorts of people; the other is that he does not always remember to speak clearly enough for the BBC to monitor his comments! The days when the General Secretary would make public appearances only on Lenin's birthday and other set-piece occasions are long gone, and now we have an energetic party leader who has a marked liking for walkabouts and 'meet the people' events. These occasions are given the most extensive media coverage, which means more work for us, and from the linguistic point of view the fact that he frequently ends up arguing, in broken and ungrammatical sentences and off the microphone, with collective farm workers who interrupt and talk at the same time as him, makes it very difficult for us to achieve the full and accurate textual translation which is part of the service we provide. Remember, too, that this is not some academic exercise we are engaged in. When Gorbachev speaks the world wants to know what he has said, and the people who rely on us for that information certainly want it fast. This can mean 10 of our monitors working flat out for several hours in order to get out not only the hot news points of his speech as it is broadcast but also the full translation as soon as possible after he stops speaking. Our consumers want the information fast, but they also of course want it accurate, and this means that the work can be very pressured at times.

Russian is not the only Soviet language we monitor: we have staff who work in most of the other major languages of the USSR, whether it be Ukrainian, Estonian, Uzbek, Kazakh or whatever. These translators too have seen their work transformed by recent developments within the country. Those, for example, who monitor the broadcasts of the Baltic republics – Estonia, Latvia and Lithuania – have experienced an explosion of information over the last two or three years. As the demands for economic, political and cultural sovereignty have risen in these republics, some quarters of the official media have played a key role in stimulating the discussion and publicising the often radical views of those who not so long ago would have been imprisoned as dissidents for voicing such demands. It came as something of a shock to some of us to discover, for example, that the English-language external service of Radio Vilnius, broadcasting from Lithuania, which once would have been a very strong candidate for the title of world's dreariest radio station, had dropped its dull propaganda and was reporting anti-government demonstrations and allegations of police brutality. The change in the tenor of domestic broadcasts is no less marked – although it is interesting to note that generally the debate is freer and more radical in the local language, as opposed to the Russian language media. This is not surprising, since much of the discontent in these republics is related to their resentment at the way they have been taken over by the Russians, and one of the most passionate issues is the question of restoring the status of the national languages in the face of Russian language domination. A few months ago the following poem appeared in an Estonian-language magazine published by the Estonian Writers' Union. It is entitled *Evening prayer*:

> Dear God, do have the courage
> to love Estonia;
> we have many Russians here:
> love them too, if you can;
> with your kindly hand
> direct them to go back;
> their minds should rejoice:
> Russia is still there!

It is difficult to imagine that appearing in any official Soviet journal before 1985!

It is in these and other outlying parts of the Soviet Union that the pressures of nationalism are being felt most keenly and expressed most openly as Gorbachev's *glasnost* lets the lid off decades of tension and resentment. Over the past year places like Armenia, Azerbaijan, Estonia, Lithuania and Georgia have become headline news, and in some cases this has meant new experiences for our monitors – for example, when the founding congress of the Lithuanian Popular Front was held over a weekend and broadcast for some 14 hours by Lithuanian state radio, our Lithuanian monitor found himself working day and night to keep up with the proceedings.

You can perhaps understand, then, that when we are recruiting new monitors we look for a particular combination of skills. First and foremost, they must really have got 'inside' the language: they must have a sound grasp of the living, idiomatic language and a precise knowledge of its grammar – we cannot afford to be caught out by 'false friends'. They must also have a wide-ranging vocabulary: we do not expect them to come with a detailed knowledge of microprocessor terminology, but on the other hand they must be capable of dealing with the language used in, say, a popular television programme about developments in the personal computer industry. We want people who can translate into good, reasonable, idiomatic English, but at the same time they have to be able to translate in a way that renders faithfully the content, meaning and style of the original: much of the material that we produce is used for detailed analysis, and too free a translation can obscure points of significance or alternatively add a significance which was not present in the original. In addition to this they must be very much at home in the contemporary culture of the country concerned, sensitive to its current affairs, aware of its historical background, and able to think and act quickly when they spot the significant, the newsworthy point in the midst of the routine material. Add to that the ability to do all this at four o'clock in the morning, listening in to catch the early morning news on Moscow Radio, and you will see that this is not your typical nine-to-five job!

Surprising though it may seem, we do actually find people who possess these qualities, and we have some very talented people on our staff. Our work is essentially responsive: we have no say in what and when they broadcast, but we have to deal with whatever they happen to throw at us. In large measure the character and scale of our own workload is determined by the broadcasters we are monitoring. Over the past four years *perestroyka*, or restructuring, in the USSR has forced a parallel *perestroyka* in our Soviet monitoring. We have had to reassess our priorities, revise our objectives and find new ways of doing our work. For us, as for the nation that coined the word, it has made life more unpredictable, and at times more bewildering, frustrating and demanding. But for all that, like them, we would rather have it like this than the way it was before.

Session 5: Report of discussion

Rapporteur: Stanley Minett, Freelance translator

In summing up the talks, the chairman commented on the responsibility that work at Caversham involved and the impact of the information explosion and mentioned *Engineering outlines* as being a useful source of background information for translators wishing to extend their specialist knowledge. He asked Mike Hollow about the discretion enjoyed by the monitors in selecting items and whether training was given in journalistic discretion. Mike replied that much had to be left to the individual, it was usually not possible to check work and they had to develop an instinct for recognising the important items.

Karin Band, a speaker on the previous day, rose to support Ben Teague's idea of consulting target language references, particularly bibliographical references published in the target language. She suggested that the client (individual or publisher) should be asked to supply them if they could as this would greatly speed up the translation process. She quoted *Index Medicus* as a valuable source of medical references and asked whether students are taught to paraphrase in their passive languages to enable them to check their understanding or to obtain definitions of terms from their clients. In a second question, Karin asked whether Mike Hollow had the opportunity of going to Russia and learned that, since he did not deal in matters of a confidential nature, no special restrictions were placed on his travel.

Betty Howell, a visitor from Canada, was interested in the personal reactions of the 'listeners' when they heard the first news of *glasnost* and *perestroyka* in 1985 and whether they believed what they were hearing. Mike Hollow said that the general reaction was one of mild astonishment and pleasure coupled with caution.

Dr Raymond Hooper, from Germany, asked Mike about shifts and the amount of time which was actually spent in translating. Mike replied that 8-hour shifts were worked, of which time about one quarter would be occupied in listening, although the proportion varied considerably according to the 'news' being broadcast at any particular time.

Aziza Molyneux-Berry, a freelance translator of Arabic, enquired who made the choice of subjects and on what basis. Mike's reply was that the choice of individual items was based on a general brief to pick out interesting and newsworthy items, especially those which related to socio-political matters, gave an insight into foreign policy, revealed the domestic situation in the country being listened to, showed changes which were taking place, or were unusual items of news (including humorous incidents).

Council member Pamela Mayorcas commented on the growing need for awareness of the need for more linguists and translators, especially in view of the tremendous increase in the amount of information which was becoming available in all languages. She invited the speakers to say whether, from their respective standpoints, they saw any increase in this awareness in those who were responsible for the distribution of information in their countries. Ben Teague very much regretted that he saw no progress in this connection in the USA and this view was endorsed by Mike with regard to the UK.

Anne Hulme, a freelance translator from Yorkshire, took up Peter Barber's mention of *Engineering outlines* and asked where they could be obtained. Peter promised to find out the current position concerning these publications and the information would be given in the ITI Bulletin.

The final contribution to the discussion came from Council member Lanna Castellano and referred to Ben Teague's observation on the need for translators to make contact with experts. She asked how one could go about this. Ben said that, apart from trying to make direct contact with individual experts in specialist fields, and particularly in the client organisation, the main answer was to try to make contacts with other translators inside and outside the client firm; they would probably be working in other languages but in the same fields and would at least understand the translator's problems. It was very much more difficult to get comments and evaluation from purchasing departments or those who were responsible for placing translation work; they often knew little about the subject matter or end-use of the translation and were frequently not interested in the science or technology involved.

Session 6: Interpreting forum

Chaired by Hilde Watson

Training the trainers of community interpreters

Lucy Collard-Abbas

Senior Lecturer, Polytechnic of Central London

First of all I would like to begin by saying that I was sorry not to have been able to attend the first day of this conference. Looking down the programme I realise that a number of the sessions are relevant to community interpreting – particularly the discussion of legal and ethical issues, the use of technology, in-service training and so on. Secondly, I think I had better own up from the start that although this is the Interpreting Forum of the conference, I am not actually an interpreter myself. But since last year I have been heavily involved in the design, running and some of the teaching of a course at the Polytechnic of Central London to 'train the trainers' of community interpreters.

What I would like to do is give a brief account of the evolution of this diploma course at PCL, with regard to the aims, content and some of the problems that have arisen. But first, what exactly do I mean by 'community interpreters'?

I do not of course mean 'community' in the sense of the European Community. A community interpreter is an interpreter trained to assist those in the community – in this case Britain – who are not native speakers of English, to gain full and equal access to statutory services (legal, health, education, local government, social services). In other words, to help those who pay for such services through their rates and taxes to make effective use of them. Up to now, much of the interpreting done in these contexts has been unsystematic. By that I mean that sometimes highly competent bilinguals have been called in to interpret; on other occasions the professional (e.g. doctor, lawyer) happened to share the same language as the patient or client. But all too often it has been a case of using the nearest person to hand, regardless of age, maturity, level of linguistic ability, level of cultural awareness. There are numerous examples of, for instance, the young child of an adult patient being called upon to act as interpreter. Therefore it is clear that demands made on community interpreters are not just linguistic: they must also have an understanding of both cultures, as well as of the context and field in which they are interpreting, for instance, a knowledge of court procedure if interpreting in a court.

Is there a difference between a community interpreter, in the sense used here, and a conference interpreter? The unfortunate, yet common, assumption is that community interpreting means interpreting at a low, amateurish level. Bearing in mind the background of some of those who have been called upon to act as interpreters – such as children – this attitude is not altogether surprising. But the whole purpose of providing training for community interpreters is precisely to change this image of the community interpreter, with its connotations of low status, lack of professionalism and the accompanying low pay.

At the Polytechnic of Central London we are trying to train community interpreters to the same level of competence and professionalism as conference interpreters, and for them to have the same awareness of the importance of working to a strict code of practice, and evolve a code of ethics appropriate to the job. It is worth remembering that it took time for conference interpreters to gain the respect and professional recognition that they now enjoy, so it will obviously take time for community interpreters to do so.

But despite the similarities, the two jobs *are* different. For instance, unlike conference interpreters, community interpreters usually have little advance warning of when they might be needed and of the context in which they will be required to interpret. Secondly, community interpreters are usually working in the physical presence of the two parties wishing to communicate. In other words, they often find themselves in an atmosphere of extreme tension, anxiety and even crisis. They are not isolated in an interpreting booth. As a result they can often find themselves being drawn towards 'taking sides'. A major aim of providing a professional training is to help the interpreter establish clear boundaries and remain unbiased in the interpreting situation. After all, the role of the professional interpreter is to interpret, and not act as legal or medical adviser.

I would now like to move on and talk about the postgraduate diploma course set up and currently being run at the Polytechnic of Central London. First, I think it is important to give some background. I know that in each of the previous two conferences organised by ITI there were papers on the Community Interpreter Project, of which the PCL course is the latest phase. But I am equally aware that some of the participants here today may not have been present at those conferences. So I apologise to those for whom I am covering old ground.

In 1983 a grant from the Nuffield Foundation made it possible to launch the Community Interpreter Project, run under the auspices of the Institute of Linguists Educational Trust and based in East Anglia. The purpose of the project is to develop models for the selection, training and use of interpreters at a local or community level. So far, the Community Interpreter Project has focused on three main courses or qualifications:

1. The Bilingual Skills Certificate – now being taught in about 25 centres throughout the UK. This certificate was designed as an access route for future interpreter training. It assesses practical, functional language skills in English and another language, at about A level standard.
2. The Certificate in Community Interpreting (CCI), whose aim is to assess community interpreters in specialised module options. The three that have

been piloted so far are: legal option (police, lower courts, probation service); local services option (social services, education welfare, local government); and health option (hospital and community care).

3. The PCL Postgraduate Diploma in Community Interpreter Training Techniques, whose aim is to 'train the trainers'.

In addition to the three courses, the Community Interpreter Project is committed to professional development. For example, interpreters who have been successful in the earlier examinations for CCI have established the British Association of Community Interpreters. Emphasis is also placed on the context of professional practice – in other words, on training key members of staff in how to work with interpreters. It is all very well making sure the community interpreter is familiar with the procedures involved in interviewing a suspect in a local police station, for instance. But it is equally essential that the police officer present is able to work comfortably and effectively through the interpreter.

As for the PCL course itself we recruited 12 students spread across three language groups, Arabic, Spanish and South Asian languages (Bengali, Urdu, Gujerati and Punjabi). We did, however, receive enquiries from people offering Turkish, Greek, Cantonese and Italian. Among the students we recruited, the majority had a BA or BSc, and some had an MA or other postgraduate qualification. Applicants were tested for linguistic ability, including memory tests to find out their suitability for interpreting work. They were also interviewed for teaching potential. When we took our final decisions we bore in mind the geographical location of the students in order to avoid the course being dominated by those living in London and the south east.

Regarding the design of the syllabus, we had constantly to keep in mind two main, parallel elements; the teacher training element and the interpreting element. At the same time we also wanted to ensure there would be an appropriate balance between theory and practice. Thus the main areas covered by the course are:

1. Applied Linguistics in Language Training, which focuses on the applications of relevant areas of linguistics to foreign or second language learning and teaching.
2. The Education and Training of Adults, which provides the theoretical underpinning needed by community interpreter trainers in their selection of appropriate and effective teaching and learning strategies. Students are introduced to pedagogical theory and learn how traditional approaches have to be adapted to the bilingual, bicultural needs of the community interpreter.
3. The Methodology of Language Teaching, including the development of teaching materials, course design and techniques for testing and assessment.
4. Principles and Practice of Interpreting and Translation, including Language Enhancement. The main aim here is not only to help students develop further their own linguistic skills, but also to pass on and enhance such skills in others.

5. A series of seminars held in conjunction with professionals from the different services, which I believe is one of the most valuable parts of the course. The aim here is to give students on the diploma course a clear, basic understanding of the structure, procedures, concepts and terminology involved in each of the main subject areas (i.e. police, court, probation, local government, education, health and social services). Equally important is the fact that student trainers actually meet representatives from the very services they will be training their own students to work with.

In conclusion, regarding course content, I should like to add that in addition to the above areas, students also go on an Interpreting Placement and a Teaching Placement.

That is the basic outline of the PCL Diploma course to 'train the trainers' of community interpreters. The course itself began in January 1989, which means that our students are nearing the end of their two terms of full-time attendance. (Between July and November 1989 they will work on individual projects.) Undoubtedly it has been one of the most fascinating and challenging courses that I personally have been involved in since I have been at PCL – and I know that many of my colleagues share similar feelings. Also I must say that we have been very fortunate to have an extremely lively, intelligent and committed group of students. But naturally there have been some problems. I think the most important lesson we have learned so far is that two terms is not long enough for a course of this nature. This may come as rather a surprise to those who have met in-service or other training courses for community interpreters that span only a few weeks. But what with the combination of theoretical and practical input, a full academic year would have been much better. This would also have allowed students to spend more time in their interpreting and teaching placements. Moreover, there is a pressing need to produce appropriate teaching materials for the kind of courses they will go out and set up – especially if one is aiming at uniformly high standards being maintained. Although the development of course materials receives attention on the diploma course I think more time would have been useful. Similarly, more time could have been spent building up comprehensive term banks – perhaps with a view to achieving eventually some kind of nationwide database to which community interpreters all over the country would have access.

From the more academic point of view, I believe that the course could have drawn additionally from other areas of linguistics – particularly socio-linguistics. A close study of issues such as bilingualism and the nature of bilingualism, as well as – for instance – code switching within a single language, would have been extremely beneficial. I am making this point because it is not enough for the community interpreter to be aware of the nature of language generally, and how it functions in a community, and how it is used in different settings and with different effect. (The interpreter often has to try and convey such linguistic awareness and understanding to the users of interpreters so that, for instance, a non-Spanish-speaking police officer is aware that English and Spanish cannot map on to one another in a word-for-word, one-to-one way. This is important because otherwise he or she may think the interpreter is elaborating or even embroidering on what has been said if the Spanish version is longer.)

The remaining issues that have emerged in the running of the course since January 1989 have been of a more practical nature, such as the difficulty of arranging for our trainers to have adequate teaching practice on appropriate courses, since at the moment so many educational institutions are facing financial difficulties and are uncertain about their future.

I would like to conclude with a few comments about the present challenges facing community interpreting in this country. First of all, it is worth noting that Britain is in fact quite behind in its development of community interpreting, especially when compared to a country like Australia, which has made great progress in this area and has allocated appropriate funds. Secondly, I believe it is essential for professional training to be made available to community interpreters so as to ensure high standards in the field. It is not difficult to imagine the potential hazards of poor interpreting. (Over ten years ago medical/psychological research was already showing a clear correlation between the high rate of misdiagnosis of mental illnesses – or retarded diagnosis – and the use of inadequately trained interpreters.) But, of course, in order to attract the most competent and committed interpreters there needs to be a major improvement in pay and working conditions. Thirdly, there is great need for co-ordination – at the national level – regarding the training of community interpreters, such that users of interpreters will know that whatever part of the country they work in, they will receive the same high-standard service.

Finally, I should add that as far as the PCL is concerned, we are going to revise the present diploma course and run it as a one-year postgraduate training from the academic year 1990/1991. This would give us the opportunity, among other things, to cater for some of the languages for which interpreters are needed but which we could not include first time round – such as Cantonese, Turkish or Greek.

Thought analysis in conference interpreting

Michael Francis

May I say how relieved I am to see that my audience is composed of more than one person: my mother. This is because of the infinite wisdom of the conference organisers, who pruned the pretentiously pedantic pomposity of the initial title of my paper: 'The practical advantages of abstract and concrete thought analysis and transfer in English/French–French/English conference interpretation', which is only marginally less deterrent than a nuclear bomb. I tried to find a more sexy title, but in the end, I had to conclude that it described almost exactly what I wanted to talk to you about. So, if you all wish to disappear now, I will quite understand.

However, before you go, I might add that I shall be delivering this paper with a little help from Rodin, Jane Fonda, Shakespeare, Maggie Thatcher, Benny Hill and a few others, but above all, it will be illustrated by my very gifted colleague Charles Cassells. So at least his caricatures will be worth a giggle or two.

The essence of conference interpretation is thought analysis. To prove my point, I think one can say that it is quite possible to train a student interpreter in a monolingual mode: English into English for example.

Take the well-known agricultural expression: 'I am not as green as I am cabbage-looking.' Interpreted into English it becomes: 'I am not as naive as I seem.'

I am not as green as I am cabbage-looking

Having defined the basis of conference interpretation as thought analysis, one has to endeavour to define thought, which is the basic ingredient of the interpreter's recipe. It is impossible to define thought without dividing it into two categories:

1. thought or ideas expressed in *abstract* terms, and
2. thought or ideas expressed in *concrete* terms.

One therefore rapidly reaches the conclusion that all conference interpreters worth their salt will have to be able rapidly to categorise the thought they are analysing and, as they are constantly under time pressure, use in their rendition whichever category is the most convenient and the most succinct.

To give you a simple example they will say either: 'The date and place of our next meeting' (abstract, 9 syllables) or: 'When and where will we next meet?' (concrete, 7 syllables).

I mention the number of syllables, as I always try to impress upon my students at Cambridge, Brussels and Mons that an interpreter should acquire the technique of expressing thought in a minimum of syllables in order not to be outdistanced by the speaker. On the whole, Anglo-Saxons express thought in concrete terms, which tend to be more monosyllabic than the terms used to express abstract ideas.

Before I go on, I had better check that the Chair has not got a copy of the International Chairperson's handbook, the edition that tells you how to stop a long-winded speaker according to nationality:

– The Italian: tie his hands behind his back. He can no longer gesticulate and will instantly be struck dumb.
– The Frenchman: simply tell him to be illogical.
– The Englishman: no Shakespeare please!

No, I don't think she has a copy. So on with the immortal bard.

Poetry being the highest verbal expression of human thought and imagination, our greatest poet will clearly express our thought in the best fashion possible. It is therefore very interesting to note with John Barton that, when Shakespeare is at his most poetic, he mainly uses concrete monosyllables.

John Barton quotes Antonio's 'In sooth, I know not why I am so sad' (10 monosyllables); Queen Margaret in *Richard III*: 'A very prey to time' (4 monosyllables, 1 polysyllable); Emilia, his wife, to Iago: 'Perchance, Iago, I will ne'er go home' (5 monosyllables, 2 polysyllables).

When Shakespeare describes the passing of time, he writes: 'To waste huge stone with little water drops' (6 monosyllables, 2 polysyllables).

To realise how right John Barton is, one merely has to rewrite Hamlet's famous soliloquy in abstract terms. 'To be or not to be, that is the question. Whether 'tis nobler in the mind to suffer the slings and arrows of outrageous fortune . . .' becomes 'Existence or its refusal is the interrogation. Is more intellectual satisfaction to be obtained by the endurance of the hazards of misfortune . . . ?' or even worse if Alexander Haig or Zbigniew Brzezinski were briefing the Pentagon: 'Which is the optimalised strategisation, existentialism or non-existentialism?'

Anglo-Saxon culture is able to express the most abstract notions in short sharp words, for instance L.P. Hartley: 'The past is a foreign country, they do things differently there'; or the 23rd Psalm (a translation, of course, but over the centuries, so well integrated in English culture):

The Lord is my shepherd; I shall not want.
He maketh me to lie down in green pastures; he leadeth me beside the still waters.
He restoreth my soul; he leadeth me in the paths of righteousness for his name's sake.
Yea, though I walk through the valley of the shadow of death, I will fear no evil; for thou art with me; thy rod and thy staff they comfort me.
Thou preparest a table before me in the presence of mine enemies; thou anointest my head with oil; my cup runneth over.
Surely goodness and mercy shall follow me all the days of my life; and I will dwell in the house of the Lord for ever.

All these quotations prove without doubt, I think, that the ethos of Anglo-Saxon culture eschews abstract expression. One could easily find as many in French to show that the Gallic language and culture espouse it.

Those of you who watched this year's Oscar ceremony, will have seen that All-American girl, Jane Fonda, no doubt in a fit of nostalgia for Roger Vadim, run riot with abstract expressions. She reeled out no less than six 'isms': autism, racism, careerism, sexism, voyeurism and tourism. After which she felt the need to crack a joke as an apology and said: 'If you want isms, we got 'em.' A British political commentator recently remarked, rather uncomfortably, that Mrs Thatcher was the first Prime Minister to be an 'ism'. In France you can become an 'isme', almost as soon as you have been elected to the parish council.

Neil Kinnock is now hitting harder at Prime Minister's Question Time, because he is starting to use short, sharp Anglo-Saxon monosyllables, not an easy task for a Welshman, though even there Maggie won the first round on the subject of football hooliganism:

KINNOCK: When it comes to football, the Honourable Lady is talking out of the back of her neck (19 syllables).
THATCHER: When it comes to talking out of the back of the neck, I can't hold a candle to my Honourable Friend (26 syllables).

Now let us return to the booth. I have strayed too far from it with Shakespeare and Jane Fonda. Put this elevating exchange into French and it becomes abstract:

KINNOCK: En parlant du football, le Premier Ministre débite des âneries (16 syllables).
THATCHER: Lorsqu'il s'agit de débiter des âneries, je ne suis vraiment pas à la hauteur (22 syllables).

It therefore seems obvious that each language and culture has its own preferred mode of expression: English, monosyllabic and concrete, French, polysyllabic and abstract. Anyone who forgets this essential truth will never be able to master English and French properly.

But to stop the Anglo-Saxons' heads swelling too much, we should never forget that French polysyllabic abstract expression can be just as succinct and often much clearer than English monosyllables. Paddy Ashdown, after the recent by-election, opens negotiations with Dr Owen and says about merging their two parties: 'We will have to discuss the practical ways of doing it' (15 syllables). In French this would be: 'Les modalités pratiques' (7 syllables).

Here, I would ask the US members of the audience not to think that I am one of those pompous insular English people, who believe that we are the only ones capable of expressing ourselves cogently in English. Take Ishmael Reed who, in his latest novels *Mumbo jumbo* and *Wreckless eyeballing*, writes English prose like Cassius Clay used to punch. Shakespeare would have been proud of him and he is one of the many fine transatlantic writers to whom we British owe an undying debt of gratitude for having reinvented the language for us. However, some of our transatlantic cousins forget the essentially concrete and monosyllabic nature of our common tongue. The male American member of the crew which flew around the world without refuelling tried to explain how he fell out of love with his female partner the more he concentrated on flying and said: 'As my mission-awareness increased, my infatuation factor diminished.'

A senior US diplomat was heard to say about *glasnost* and *perestroyka* recently: 'We are witnessing an extraordinary process of democratisation and economic marketisation.' It sounds good but what does it mean?

But we Brits are just as good at resorting to abstract verbiage, when we want to be deliberately vague and evasive. A marvellous example of this is to be found in an episode of *Yes, Prime Minister*. Sir Humphrey's skeleton (£40 million, wasted on a completely fatuous scheme) has left its cupboard and he has to own up. He says:

> The identity of the official, whose alleged responsibility for this hypothetical oversight has been the subject of recent discussion, is *not* shrouded in quite such impenetrable obscurity as certain previous disclosures would lead you to assume. Not to put too fine a point on it, the individual in question is, it may surprise you to learn, one whom your present intelocutor is in the habit of defining by means of the perpendicular pronoun.

Interpretation: 'It was my fault' (4 monosyllables).

The only clear part of this speech is the phrase: 'not to put too fine a point on it' (9 monosyllables). I did not have time to count the abstract polysyllables. I merely wished to ask him if his pendigestatory interludicum facilitated his velocitous extramuralisation.

Bilingual or biactive interpreters, working into and from French and English, therefore, have to be two-headed monsters; one English and one French head.

They also have to change gear constantly from concrete to abstract moods as they switch languages. Here are a few examples straight out of the booth:

- 'We don't know who were caught up in the casualties' (13 syllables)
- 'Nous ignorons l'identité des victimes' (11 syllables)

- 'Les destinataires des commentaires' (9 syllables)
- 'Where the comments will go' (6 syllables)

- 'La qualité des photocopies se dégrade' (12 syllables)
- 'The photocopies become fainter' (9 syllables)

- 'Vous êtes priés de décliner vos nationalités' (15 syllables)
- 'You are invited to say which countries you represent' (14 syllables)

- 'Les exercices sont des processus d'apprentissage' (13 syllables)
- 'Exercises are there for learning' (9 syllables).

By using the technique of abstract-concrete mode transfer according to the language they are working into, interpreters can nearly always prune out 10–15 per cent of the syllables. This is, however, slightly more difficult when translating into French than into English. After all, President Botha had a 'stroke' in English (1 syllable) and a 'congestion cérébrale' in French (7 syllables).

It is essential to remain true to the ethos of the language, and to make my point I would like to return to my first example. 'The date and place of the next meeting' (9 syllables) becomes in concrete 'When and where we will next meet' (7 monosyllables). If you put it into abstract French, it becomes: 'date et lieu de la prochaine réunion' (11 syllables). But it becomes longer, more clumsy and unnatural if you put it into concrete French: 'Quand et où nous nous réunirons la prochaine fois' (13 syllables).

Let us return to our two-headed monster, the bilingual interpreter. Two heads, or four if you add a concrete and abstract one to the already existing French and English heads; but, like Polyphemus, one eye – the mind's eye, which sees through the words to perceive the meaning.

I was recently interpreting the following text on the democratisation of the decision-making process. 'For over three decades after the Second World War, the power structure for policy-making in many Western European countries was a steep pyramid.' A basically abstract expression with one concrete element: the pyramid. My mind's eye very clearly saw the pyramid and I built my interpretation round it.

But beware of falling into traps. Remember you only have one mind's eye. For instance 'fish farming' becomes 'pisciculture' in French. Your mind's eye must see one concept, not a fish and a farm. Here the ignorant Anglo-Saxon must see a tank full of fish and not think that pisciculture is a new and revolutionary method of urine analysis.

But what are we interpreters to do about interpreting humour? The problem is that the English and the French do not laugh at the same things or in the same way. I was unfortunate enough to test some of my students in Mons in the translation of humour and quoted two verbal caricatures of Sir Geoffrey Howe which I found entertaining. Sir Geoffrey was described as 'charismatically boring and accommodatingly firm' to be translated into abstract French as 'd'un ennui charismatique et d'une fermeté souple'. None of my students got the joke. Being Cartesian, they felt that you were either charismatic or boring, either accommodating or firm.

One can understand how even the toughest and most experienced interpreter is turned to jelly when the speaker says: 'Now, ladies and gentlemen, I am going to tell you a joke.' The fact remains that only straight jokes can be translated. Even Benny Hill sounds ridiculous when dubbed. The furthest you can go is a basic if

*Charismatically boring
and accommodatingly firm!*

subtle smile at things like: 'I knew Doris Day before she was a virgin', or the male chauvinist pig's ploy to end all ploys: 'I don't mind letting women think they are my betters, as long as they don't think they are my equals'.

I have noticed, over the years, that the general public's attitude to my profession is ambivalent. An interpreter is either viewed as being part of the furniture, a sort of linguistic tap one turns on to get hot and cold running translation or, more flatteringly, as a universal genius with an intimate knowledge of 35 languages and 250 minor dialects and an IQ which makes Einstein seem a mental deficient. Both views are, of course, far from the mark. However, I hope that my paper has convinced you that the latter is the less inaccurate.

Session 6: Report of discussion

Rapporteur: Rita Day, Freelance, London

Karin Band commented to Michael Francis that thought analysis is valid for translators too, not just for interpreters. Syllable counting is not very profitable (although she agreed that interpreters – and translators – should look for the briefest way of putting things, if possible). The French language is becoming much more terse in the practical sphere and can often be significantly shorter than English. Anglo-Saxon is a French concept that puts together British and American English. She said that the problem with American English is that it sometimes works at a very concise level (to 'mickeymouse') and sometimes so verbose a level that it may be difficult for the British to understand.

Michael Francis replied that it was absolutely true that thought analysis is a must not only for interpreters and promised to check his script to make sure this was not what he had said. Even children going to a kindergarten must learn thought analysis, he said and he apologised if translators felt he was treating them differently. He agreed about what was said on the 'Americans'. He pointed out that his German was practically non-existent but had been told that the Americans are verbose in a similar way to the Germans. One of the most brilliant speakers he had worked for was Henry Kissinger who speaks English with a German accent and also speaks perfect German but few people can actually express themselves in such a concise and direct way, he said. He thought that people use verbose sentences in order to confuse the issue. Senior diplomats are taught to speak in such a way as not to give anything away so that what they say can be interpreted in many different ways.

Stella Cragie, of the Interpreters' School, Naples, asked Lucy Collard how the question of dialects in community interpreting for languages such as Italian, Arabic, etc. was tackled. In many cases, e.g. Neapolitan, there is an enormous difference compared with the 'classical' standard. Were special courses designed to include dialects?

Lucy Collard agreed that this was a very big problem, and it would take a 10-year course to get students acquainted with dialects. There is no Italian on the course but in the case of Arabic they try and make sure that they cater for the majority of dialects that are to be found in Britain. With Arabic they do not give classical training because often students will be dealing with people who have not even been to school in their own country. It was a major problem, and one not easily solved. However, she felt that the simpler type of language was no solution and that they were lucky in that they know the type of community for which they are training. But in the case of Spanish, for example, they often have people from South America who are professors of universities and very sophisticated so interpreters have to be able to cope with them. These were problems they make trainers aware of since it is what they will find in the day-to-day reality.

Jane Taylor asked Lucy Collard how one could sensitise local authorities to the need to train the trainers of community interpreters and to get them to place it towards the top of their priorities.

Lucy Collard agreed that this was a very important area. They have one person who deals with the financial side of the enterprise, Ann Corsellis, who could unfortunately not be present; she is very active in doing just that. As to the background of students, it was very mixed. Two of them have been seconded to the course and are receiving regular salaries from their employers; one comes from Scotland, the other one from the Midlands. Scotland is doing very well and there they are far more aware of the problem than we are. For other students the situation is different, reflecting the fact that this is a low priority job for authorities. Conference interpreters are moving in an international field and diplomatic incidents could arise from badly handled situations. However, a community interpreter dealing with a mother in hospital gets lower priority, for instance.

Hilde Watson remarked that Ann Corsellis is a magistrate and is at the receiving end of interpreting services; she has, therefore, a lot of knowledge and this is why her team has got off to a good start.

Gunnar Lemhagen, of Stockholm University, Institute for Interpretation and Translation Studies, said that in Sweden the need for community interpreters had been urgent for many years. They started their first experimental courses in 1968 but they still had problems when it came to the number of interpreters they can train and the languages they can offer. Some 7,000 people in Sweden are registered as community interpreters but few have proper training. He asked to know the number of community interpreters in Britain and how many have received training.

Lucy Collard replied that she could not give any such figures for Britain, as there is no such systematisation. Often interpreters in Britain go to the local Police Station and let them know that they could help in that particular area. Often it is also assumed that if a person is bilingual he or she must automatically be an intepreter. She hoped we would improve on this situation. She stressed the injustice in the fact that there are people who are willing and would be able to become community interpreters but that training is not available. If we were to look at the people registered in the various areas of the country, she said, this would not provide any indication of their training. There were some possibilities for day release courses, but these are normally very short.

Janet Fraser, of the Polytechnic of Central London, put a question to both Lucy Collard and Michael Francis: when faced with the problem of translating/ interpreting cultural concepts did they:

– try to explain them, which could take some time
– try to find a (possibly misleading) equivalent in the target language

– educate the user and leave them in the original language, e.g. *glasnost?*

Lucy Collard replied that for the community interpreters there was one advantage – one among the many disadvantages they have to face – and this was to know exactly the context of the field they were dealing with. For instance, in a medical centre you come up against a term such as 'health visitor'. Everybody appears to know what it means but if you try to translate it into the language of a country where such a concept does not exist, you are quite likely to create confusion, so you must keep the concept in the original language. They have the advantage that the person for whom they are interpreting is familiar with the system and will know exactly what this concept means, so their students are taught to keep this kind of concept in the original language.

Michael Francis, whose particular field is simultaneous conference interpreting in French and English, also said that there was no time to go in for explanations, but French and English cultures were different but similar, and therefore this was not really a major problem. He felt that one of the most tricky things happens right at the beginning of a meeting when the chairman introduces the speaker and tells us all what he has done and that, for instance, he is the warden of Robinson College, Cambridge. To try and put all that into French loses its meaning, so the best is to leave it as such because there is no time to explain what it really means. You just have to assume that it will be understood and keep your fingers crossed.

Hilde Watson said that the same problem arose between English and American when, for instance, the headmaster of a school becomes the principal.

Mansour Awad, a court interpreter/translator from France commented that there is a problem with Arabic dialects, where someone born in Egypt, for instance, cannot interpret for an Algerian or a Moroccan, so an interpreter of the same country is needed. In Paris there was the Ecole d'Etudes Orientales. Dialects are taught there but this is dangerous too because you come up against the same problem. If you learn one North African dialect, you will not be understood by the people living in the neighbouring country. There was also the added problem, he said, that sometimes, even if an individual from Morocco, for instance, understands Egyptian, he will refuse to speak to the interpreter.

Lucy Collard replied that this highlighted a major problem. To add to the confusion sometimes the same words have different meanings in different dialects. She said that in London the School of Oriental and African studies does teach some dialects.

Roger Fletcher, freelance community interpreter, made a comment to Lucy Collard, in answer to Gunnar Lemhagen's question, that there were about 30 people who have obtained the Community Interpreter Certificate. There were also conference interpreters working in this field, but almost everybody else in this field is untrained or self-taught. Lucy Collard pointed out that the course that leads to the Community Interpreter Certificate at the moment was just a pilot one which should lead to a properly established system.

John Craddock, freelance translator, asked Michael Francis whether he had not misused the word Anglo-Saxon when he really meant British. Michael Francis replied that he had been away from Britain since 1961 and his English had been polluted by the French into grouping all English speakers into one. It was probably fair to say that if you all spoke the same language your mind is probably working in the same way. He felt that the best way to describe this was that the Anglo-Saxons speak in a concrete way and the Americans were very good at doing it too, so he did not see why John Craddock was unhappy at the use of this word.

Session 7: The profession

Chaired by Chris Percival

After Geoffrey Kingscott's paper 'The Literature of Translation', the chairman welcomed the representatives of a number of overseas professional associations, who brought greetings to ITI and then gave a brief account of their organisation, followed by a general discussion. They included Jennifer Mackintosh of the Association Internationale des Interprètes de Conférence, Fernanda Mello of the Associazione Italiana Traduttori e Interpreti, John Graham of the Bundesverband der Dolmetscher und Übersetzer, Betty Howell of the Société des Traducteurs du Québec, Manfred Schubert of the Vereinigung der Sprachmittler der DDR, Eva Eie of the Norsk Oversetterforening, and David Lord of the Société Francaise des Traducteurs.

The literature of translation

Geoffrey Kingscott

Praetorius Ltd

This is an ambitious, some would say foolhardy, attempt to survey all that has been written on the subject of translation and interpreting, in a short space.

PORTRAYAL IN LITERATURE

I have even decided to widen the net still further, and look at how translators and interpreters are shown in fictional literature. I have not found any previous documentation on this particular subject. I am afraid my survey is Anglo-centred, but I would welcome any indication as to omissions, or treatment of our professions in literature other than English. My researches turned up only four works where a translator or interpreter is a major character and is shown exercising his or her profession. I have not included books where other types of linguists are involved, such as Charlotte Brontë's *Villette*, where the heroine teaches English in Brussels, or Malcolm Bradbury's *Rites of passage*, where the much put-upon main character is a linguistics lecturer.

Arthur Conan Doyle's *The Greek interpreter* is one of the Sherlock Holmes stories; two quotations illustrate something of the professional activity of those times.

> Mr Melas is a Greek by extraction, as I understand, and he is a remarkable linguist. He earns his living partly as an interpreter in the courts, partly by acting as guide to any wealthy Oriental who may visit the Northumberland Avenue hotels . . . .

> I interpret all languages, or nearly all, but as I am a Greek by birth, and with a Grecian name, it is with that particular tongue that I am principally associated. For many years I have been the chief Greek interpreter in London, and my name is very well known in the hotels.

As far as I know, interpreting for wealthy visitors is no longer a major activity for our profession. The Greek interpreter is hired in a case which involved some skulduggery. The story was included in the current Sherlock Holmes television series.

The book by Michael Frayn, *The Russian interpreter*, is set in Moscow, and the interpreter of the title has to interpret advances made by someone he dislikes to the lady he is secretly in love with. John Hale's *The whistleblower* (made into a film with Michael Caine and Nigel Havers) is about a Russian translator at an institution obviously based on GCHQ at Cheltenham, where the character played in the film by Nigel Havers is killed quite early in the book because he was about to reveal something he considers unethical. There is, of course, an ethical question both in *The Greek interpreter* and *The whistleblower* about whether interpreters dealing with highly confidential matters have the right to make their own judgements about whether to reveal them to the world, but this dilemma is not really explored.

I cannot resist, too, quoting an example in Trollope (*Phineas Finn*) of interpreting (the author calls it translation) taking place, though no detail is given of the interpreter. The passage, however, attracts me because of the description of the tiresome know-all whom all interpreters have met, the one who must show off his language knowledge even though interpreters are present. The passage describes a sitting of the potted peas committee of the House of Commons.

> The proof was naturally slow, as the evidence was given in German, and had to be translated into English. And the work of the day was much impeded by a certain member who unfortunately spoke German, who seemed to be fond of speaking German before his brethren of the Committee, and who was curious as to agriculture in Holstein generally. The chairman did not understand German, and there was a difficulty in checking this gentleman and in making him understand that his questions were not relevant to the issue.

So far we have not seen a great deal about how the profession is actually exercised, but I would like to draw your attention to something much more relevant, and that is the play *Interpreters*, by Ronald Harwood, best known for another play *The dresser*. *Interpreters*, which was staged in the West End in November 1985 with Edward Fox and Maggie Smith in the leading roles, interweaves the practice of interpreting into the drama. Two major scenes show interpreting actually taking place. The Russian diplomat portrayed speaks only Russian on stage, and Edward Fox had to learn how to speak the Russian-speaking part of his lines sufficiently well to carry conviction. A revived love affair between the English interpreter (the Maggie Smith part) and the Russian (the Edward Fox part), acquires serious political consequences, and the interpreters are compelled to interpret the discussion of their own affair (cf the Michael Frayn work), leading to considerable dramatic tension. The play is now available in book form, published by the Amber Lane Press, Oxford.

For the reader's convenience I have added here suggestions made from the floor or notified to me after the conference: James Grady, *Six days of the condor* (mentioned from the floor by Ben Teague; Robert Redford took the part of the translator who saves the world, when a film *Three days of the condor* was made of the novel); Graham Greene, *Dr Fischer of Geneva* (mentioned from the floor by Lanna Castellano; Florence Mitchell, London, added this note – Alan Bates took the role in the film, as the translator in a chocolate factory; one never saw him at work. It was sympathetic to this way of life, and ironic, since he was in love with the factory's millionaire owner); Doris Lessing, *The summer before the dark* (suggested by Karin Band, Surbiton, who commented: 'I don't know where the good lady got her story line from, but as a working conference interpreter, I know that it is rubbish.' The novel was reviewed in the *AIIC Bulletin*, Vol. XV, no. 4, November 1987). Florence Mitchell also mentioned in a note passed to me after the conference that a novel in French by Christine Arnothy revolves round an incident where an interpreter in a booth forgets that the microphone is on when he says 'Quel con, celui-là', while another French novel, by Vita Hessel, *Les temps difficiles*, has a Unesco translator as its main character.

I would just like to pause to reflect on the comparative paucity, with the exception of the above, of translator and interpreter characters in fiction, and on how inter-lingual communication is dealt with in fiction. This is apart from cases where educated people converse in a *lingua franca* (Latin in the Middle Ages, cf Umberto Eco, *The name of the rose*); later French (Shakespeare, you will remember, has a whole scene in French in *Henry V* and expects his audience to follow it, while in Tolstoy's *War and peace* Russian aristocrats talk French to their conquerors); and English in the modern world.

I have identified three ways in which novelists deal with the translingual problem.

One is to present the hero as a super-linguist himself: take Richard Hannay, in the John Buchan novels, who in *Greenmantle* can pass himself off as a German in the heart of Germany in the First World War, while his colleague Sandy Arbuthnot does the same as a Turkish bandit in Turkey; in more recent fiction, Flashman in the Flashman series of novels by George Macdonald Fraser, at various times masters Pushtu in Afghanistan, various Indian languages sufficiently well to pass for a native in different parts of the sub-continent, the Red Indian language Apache, and Chinese, including its dialects, not to speak of various European languages. To be fair, though, while masquerading as a Danish prince (in *Royal Flash*), he does not quite manage to convince the prince's oldest friend, who deliberately asks something difficult, and for the first time Flashman has to admit, *Jag forstar icke*!

Well, here we are gathered in this hall, the super-linguists of Britain, and we know that masquerading in another language, certainly in more than one, is often more than we could get away with; we know the novelists are having us on; but until the ignorance of the general public about language is remedied, there is little we can do about it.

Another fictional device, or not so much a device as sheer lack of imagination, is not to realise that the problem exists. The most amusing example I found of this was in '*Planet of the apes*', where, many centuries into the future, the apes have evolved to take over the Earth. And what sort of language have they evolved to communicate in? Surprise, surprise, mid-20th-century American English, so there is no difficulty in communicating with the spacemen strayed over from our own era. Incidentally, not only is what happens linguistically improbable, it is also physiologically impossible for apes to produce human speech, but we'll let that pass.

Yet another device, which they are fond of in science fiction, is to have miracle machines so that we humanoids have no difficulty in understanding the four-headed Bogadons from the Blue Planet of a distant galaxy. The best example comes from that glorious spoof of the genre, *The hitch-hiker's guide to the Galaxy*, by Douglas Adams (published 1979 by Pan), where to understand the Vogons all you have to do is put a fish in your ear – a special kind of fish, of course.

> The Babel fish is small, yellow and leech-like, and probably the oddest thing in the Universe. It feeds on brainwave energy received not from its own carrier but from those around it. It absorbs all unconscious mental frequencies from this brainwave energy to nourish itself with. It then excretes into the mind of its carrier a telepathic matrix formed by combining the conscious thought frequencies with nerve signals picked up from the speech centres of the brain which has supplied them. The practical upshot of this is that if you stick a Babel fish in your ear you can instantly understand anything said to you in any form of language. The speech patterns you actually hear decode the brainwave matrix which has been fed into your mind by your Babel fish.

If you put that into a brochure promoting machine translation, there would be customers who would believe it.

HISTORY AND DESCRIPTIONS OF PROFESSIONAL ACTIVITY

Very little has been written about the history of our profession. But the CTIC, the Canadian equivalent of the ITI, has done it as far as Canada is concerned. Jean Delisle, *La traduction au Canada/Translation in Canada, 1534 to 1984*, published by the Ottawa University Press, 1987, is an excellent publication, which covers not only history, but also gives details of translator training and translator associations in Canada, and a comprehensive bibliography of books, articles, etc. appertaining to translation in Canada.

In the historical section, however, which took 15 years of research, we start at the very beginnings of Canada, with the capture by Jacques Cartier in 1534 of two Iroquois Indians, who were taken to France to be taught French to act as interpreters for future expeditions. We read about the early missionaries to the Indian tribes and about communication during the Anglo-French wars, and so on up to the present day. The historical section of the book ends with the 1984 discussions to create the FIT regional association for North America.

It was the historical section of this book, particularly those early incidents, that set me wondering whether anything similar could be produced for Britain. I therefore, as my modest contribution, had a look at Caesar's *Gallic wars* to see if anything similar to the Cartier experience occurred here. In the book there is a lot of communication going on with the British tribes: envoys are received, hostages are exchanged, Caesar gives a speech to the British chiefs reproaching them for their faithlessness – the chiefs reply that it was someone else's fault (as British political chiefs usually do); but nowhere do we discover in what language these exchanges took place, or whether interpreters were involved! So I don't even know where we would start for a history of translation in Britain!

I might mention at this point two books which I have not myself read or seen, but which are said to describe translating and interpreting with the Red Indians during the opening up of North America. One is a fictionalised biography of one of the early Jesuit missionaries to the Indian tribes, Etienne Brûlé, called *No man's brother* by Charles Ewert, published in Canada (Avon Books, Scarborough) in 1984. The other, which came up in my bibliographical searches, is Jack Long, *Voyages and travels of an Indian interpreter and trader*, published in London in 1791.

Moving closer to our times, I know that David and Margareta Bowen of the University of Georgetown in the United States were engaged at one time on a history of translating and interpreting at the Nuremberg War Crimes Tribunals, which gave such a major impetus to the profession, and which were held after the end of the Second World War. I do not know how far that historical project has advanced, but I have read one of their articles describing how Göring, who knew English quite well, intervened to challenge the interpretation of *Endlösung* (sometimes *Gesamtlösung*) as 'final solution' (of the Jewish question), aware of the chilling implication of the phrase in English.

The early history of the American Translators Association has been told in a book by Bernie Bierman, *A translator-warrior speaks* (published by Information Resources Management, New York, 1987), which presents the story from his own personal and very maverick viewpoint.

The history of machine translation has been told several times, but by general consensus the definitive work on the subject – at least up to 1986, when it was published – is the work by John W. Hutchins, *Machine translation, past, present and future* (Ellis and Horwood, Chichester, 1986). For what is probably the best bibliography in print on machine translation you should turn to a book edited by Jonathan Slocum, *Machine translation systems* (Cambridge University Press, 1988). Mention of this bibliography will, I hope, excuse me for not going further into the huge but scattered literature on machine translation. One problem is that the field is moving so quickly and so I ought to quote at least one other work, which has appeared since the Slocum book, and which has a less comprehensive bibliography but which has some items in it which appeared too late for Slocum; this is *Machine translation, linguistic characteristics of MT systems and general methodology of evaluation*, by Lehrberger and Bourbeau (John Benjamins, Amsterdam, 1988).

Before leaving the subject of the history of translation, I would like to mention some books mentioned in bibliographies, but which I have not seen myself, and which may be out of print: L.G. Kelly, *Translation – theory and practice in the West*, 1971; Carlo Lapuci, *Dal volgarizzazione alla traduzione*, Florence, 1973; Bonnerot and others, *Chemins de la traduction*, Didier, Paris, 1963; D. Gouadec, *Comprendre et traduire – techniques de la version*, Bordas, Paris, 1974; J. Guillemin-Fleischer, *Syntaxe comparée du français et de l'anglais – problèmes de traduction*, Ophrys, Paris, 1981. Any further details on these would be welcome.

I should also mention there is a long-standing FIT project for an *Histoire générale de la traduction*, but I have not heard of any progress made. There was also a survey of the translation profession, *Better translation for better communications*, by the Bureau Marcel van Dijk, Belgium, published by Pergamon in 1983, but I found it quite unrevealing.

Many of the FIT member organisations publish directories of their members. In the UK there have been at least two attempts to publish independent directories, one by a publisher called Pond in the 1960s, now long out of print, and a current one by the Merton Press. An international directory by a New York publisher, Bowker, appeared in the early 1970s. The most remarkable directory of all that I have seen, and for a minor language, Slovene, at that, is *Slovenski leksikon novejsiega prevajanja*, by Janko Moder, published in Yugoslavia, which gives the biographies and publications of no less than 3,000 Slovene translators, past and present.

Graham Pascoe, of Munich, has drawn my attention to Dr Paul Schmidt's *Statist auf diplomatischer Bühne*, 1948: these are the memoirs of a man who was Hitler's interpreter at occasions such as the Munich encounter with Neville Chamberlain. A less dramatic but more language-oriented tale was told by Bible translator J.B. Phillips, who in 1984 published his autobiography, *The price of success*, publisher Hodder and Stoughton (success, that is, in finding the *mot juste* or right turn of phrase).

I have also been told about a book, *Lanterns over Pinchgut*, by Anne Kerr, an autobiography with a large part about her life as an interpreter before marrying Sir John Kerr (a recent Governor-General of Australia). Frances Edmonds, wife of former Test cricketer Phil Edmonds, also sometimes refers to an earlier interpreting career in her books about her experiences, described with wry humour. A much sourer viewpoint is that of an Italian translator called Biancardi, whose book *La vita agra* makes clear what a rotten life translators have. Raoul Journeau, *Le 'business' de la traduction* (Guy Maheux, Montreal, 1981), is another diatribe about the unsatisfactory way translators are treated.

A Spanish writer called Julio-Cesar Santoyo wrote *El delito de traducir* (published by Universidad de León), drawing attention to some of the many errors and misunderstandings translators have committed over the centuries. Another oddity is a book which appeared in Germany in 1985 by Hans Grassegger called *Sprachspiel und Übersetzung* (publisher, Stauffenberg Verlag, Tübingen), about the translation of word-play, with special reference to translation of the Asterix books into German.

MANUALS

There is not all that much available in the way of practical manuals. The one that springs to mind is *The translator's handbook*, published by Aslib and edited by ITI's own Catriona Picken. The second edition is now being prepared. This book does not tell you how to translate, but gives you all the information you can reasonably need about translation as a career and as a professional activity.

There is a small number of books supposedly telling you how to translate. The earliest one, and I came across frequent references to it in later publications, dates back to 1791 and is called *Essays on the principles of translation*, by Alexander Tytler. Ian Finlay wrote a book, *Translating*, in 1971 in the Teach Yourself series published by the English Universities Press, but it is now out of print. The best practical guide I know is really for French translators; it is a book by Claude Bédard, whom some of you may know, and is called *La traduction technique, principes et pratique*, and came out in 1986 (published by Linguatech, Canada). We really need something like it in English. Still in French, someone called Jean St-Georges did bring out a book called *Notes de traduction* in 1954 (published by La Presse Canadienne), but it is of limited application, being an aide-mémoire for press agency translators.

You get a few hints on translating from French and Spanish in a book by Frederick Fuller, confusingly also called *A translator's handbook* (Colin Smythe, London, 1984), but it is rather unstructured, and is mostly about false friends. In Italian we have ITI member Stella Cragie's, 'Translation skills', *Manuale di traduzione*, published by Fiorentina, Naples, in 1984, on the theory and practice of translation, intended for university level students.

There is a book called *A textbook of translation*, by Professor Peter Newmark, which came out last year (1988), publisher Prentice Hall International (a follow-up to his celebrated *Approaches to translation*, Pergamon, Oxford, 1981) and which, in view of the high reputation of the author, and its title and professed aim, ought to have been the essential guide for the English translator. Well, it did get favourable reviews – with just one exception – and it won the British Association of Applied Linguistics prize. I still feel, however – I was the writer of one unfavourable review – that the book is unstructured and not particularly helpful, though I have to admit that Professor Newmark wrote to me after my hostile, not to say unpleasantly sarcastic, review a very friendly, and also very cogently argued, letter defending his book. His book does deal with some of the nitty-gritty of translation, such as the translation of titles, or lexical lacunae, and such information is difficult to find elsewhere, except in Bédard.

In German there is a book by Wolf Friederich called *Technik des Übersetzens*, originally published in 1969 by Max Hueber Verlag, Munich, 'eine systematische Anleitung für das Übersetzen ins Englische und ins Deutsche für Unterricht und Selbststudium' which has been popular in Germany (it went to at least three editions) but which to me seems discursive and over-theoretical. In Italian there is Emanuele Calò's *Manuale del traduttore* (Edizioni Scientifiche, Naples, 1984), but this is more concerned with matters such as copyright laws and agreements with publishers that with how translations are done. Incidentally, in *Language Monthly* no. 10 (July 1984), Emanuele Calò wrote about books available in Italian on translation; the article was entitled 'Appunti sulla recente bibliografia italiana in tema di traduzione'.

A book by Paul V. Hendrickx in 1971 called *Simultaneous interpreting – a practice book* (published by Longman) is now out of print, perhaps fortunately, because it was roundly condemned in reviews at the time as being simplistic. The work of Professor Seleskovitch, such as *Interpréter pour traduire* (Didier, Paris, 1984), is more useful, though it should perhaps be considered under the heading of translating and interpreting theory. A book which appears in bibliographies, but which I have not seen, nor have I seen any reviews, is J. Maillot, *La traduction scientifique et technique*, Eyrolles, 1981.

The American Translators Association, and all honour is due to them, have launched what they call a Scholarly Monography series, in hard covers, under the general editorship of Marilyn Gaddis Rose. The first volume to be issued, in 1987, was *Translation excellence: assessment, achievement, maintenance*. In 1988 they published volume II, *Technology as translation strategy*, with 33 separate articles, including three by UK-based contributors, John Hutchins, Veronica Lawson and myself. Volume III, projected for this year (1989), is to be on translator and interpreter training.

In my opinion, however, there is a book still waiting to be written, at least in English, of useful information concerning the best practice to be followed in the translation process itself.

CONFERENCE PROCEEDINGS

Descriptions of professional translation and interpreting activity can be found in the fastest growing body of literature covering our profession, conference proceedings.

In the United Kingdom we have the proceedings of the Translating and the Computer conference series, with which the ITI is closely associated, and which started the year following a major conference in Luxembourg in 1977. Organised by the Commission of the European Communities, the proceedings of this were published in two volumes (*Overcoming the language barrier*, Luxembourg, May 3–6, 1977, Verlag Dokumentation, Munich). The Translating and the Computer conference proceedings are published each year by Aslib (proceedings of some of the earlier conferences in the series were published by North Holland, Amsterdam). Proceedings have also been published since the 1970s of the biennial COLING international conferences, mainly concerned with the more theoretical, computational linguistics side of machine translation.

The American and Canadian translator associations, and of course ITI, publish the proceedings of their conferences, as does FIT, the international association. If we exclude FIT, not so much has come out of the continent, where conferences are usually reported in the newsletters of the associations rather than as separate books. The French, however, are starting to move into this field, with the publication in 1987 of the proceedings of the *Journées européennes de la traduction* and, more recently, of two SFT seminars held in conjunction with Expolangues 1988. And the Internationale Vereinigung Sprache und Wirtschaft, which covers both translation and business language learning, has begun publishing the proceedings of its annual conferences. Further afield, I have come across a 1981 publication of 98 pages from Chile, *Teoría y práctica de la traducción, primer encuentro internacional de traductores* (published by the Instituto de Letras, Universidad Católica de Chile, which includes a paper by the celebrated Eugene Nida).

It is all proliferating fast, and there is an urgent need to record it all on computer, a database of everything published on translating and interpreting. The Canadians have done it for Canada.

JOURNALS

Following on from conference proceedings, this is perhaps the best place to deal with journals on translating and interpreting. There are, to begin with, the newsletters and journals of the translating and interpreting organisations, such as our own *ITI News*, or the *Aslib Technical Translation Group Newsletter*. In France they have *Traduire*, with often interesting material but depressingly printed,* in Germany *Mitteilungsblatt* (rather heavy going), in the United States *The ATA Chronicle* (now a very lively publication under its witty editor Ted Crump), in Switzerland *Hieronymus*, in Mexico *El Traductor*, etc. Internationally there is the FIT journal *Babel* (rather over-theoretical, to my taste), and the *AIIC Bulletin*. My own favourites at the moment are the Finnish translators' journal *Kääntäjä*, the only one I know in newspaper format, and very well laid out, the Netherlands' *Van Taal tot Taal*, which seems to have a high proportion of serious articles well-written and well-presented, and *Circuit*, journal of the Quebec translators' association, which is professionally presented, with attractive layout, and has well-researched articles.

But of course on the stocks, and soon to come down the slipway, is ITI's new flagship, the *Professional Translator and Interpreter*, under the editorship of Mike Shields.

There are of course general language magazines which do have occasional articles on translation, such as *The Linguist* of the Institute of Linguists, and *Multilingua* (though the latter journal has recently become very theoretical) but it would widen my brief immeasurably if I tried to cover them all.

To move on to the independent journals, the longest-running of all, both over 30 years old, are *Lebende Sprachen* and *Meta*. The former is published in Germany by Langenscheidt, in collaboration with the BDÜ, and has good theoretical articles, authoritative reviews and glossaries on diverse subjects. The latter is produced at the University of Montreal in Canada. Instead of printing such articles as happen to come in, as many academic journals do, *Meta* often chooses a theme for an issue and commissions articles on that theme. Examples are Bible translating (vol. 32, no. 1, March 1987) or conference interpreting (vol. 30, no. 1, March 1985, with probably the fullest bibliography published on the subject), or terminotics in vol. 32, no. 2, June 1987. (If, like me, you wonder what the term 'terminotics' means, I think it is a piece of Canadian English, a *calque* of *terminotique* from French-Canadian, and means 'study of terminology'.)

A heavily theoretical journal for machine translation is *Computers and Translation*.

In France there was for about five years in the early 1980s *La Revue du Traducteur*, a heroic effort by one man, Claude Cornilleau, which eventually succumbed to commercial reality, i.e. the losses were no longer sustainable. I much regretted its disappearance, but no-one else seems to have noticed, for I have never seen it written about anywhere except by me. Then there was *Language Monthly*, which I published and edited here in the UK for five years between 1983 and 1988 before I, in my turn, had to succumb to commercial reality. It was merged into *Language Technology*, which looks at languages, I think it is fair to say, from the viewpoint of the computer-minded. It is true that many former *Language Monthly* subscribers rebelled at their *LM* being replaced with *LT*, and I was quite taken aback at the time by the vehemence some of them expressed. Like many people, I find *Language Technology's* style and layout, shall we say, idiosyncratic, but it provides insights and information available nowhere else, and it gets better with each issue. Some of its recent features, such as those on speech recognition, or language in the European Communities, provide real in-depth treatment of the subject. In any case, out of the upheavals of 1988 there emerged a new journal, *Language International*, more attuned to the translator who is not mad about computers, so now there is something for everyone.

Finally there is a number of largely theoretical journals, often connected with a particular university or translation school, such as *Jerome Quarterly*, from Georgetown University in Washington; *Parallèles*, from the Geneva Ecole de Traduction et d'Interprétation; *Translation Review*, from the University of Texas at Dallas; *TTR* (Traduction, Terminologie, Rédaction), from the University of Quebec at Trois-Rivières; and *TextContext* from the University of Heidelberg.

Translation studies, or *traductologie*, are now a major concern in Canadian universities, and there is now a Canadian association of translation studies, with its own newsletter.

THEORY

This brings us to translation theory proper, which is an immense field of its own. Translation theory, as distinct from translation practice, has a huge literature starting, as far as I can judge, with Cicero in 50 BC. Fortunately, however, I feel I can dispose of the first 2,000 years very quickly, since all the various writers on the subject, Cicero, St Jerome, Martin Luther, Dryden and many others, were all in effect re-inventing the wheel. When I say re-inventing the wheel I mean that all these authors found, somewhat to their surprise, that to translate successfully, you did not translate literally, word for word, but you tried to convey the sense of the source text.

As St Jerome put it: 'Ego enim non solum fateor, sed libera voce profiteor me in interpretatione Graecorum absque scripturus sanctis, ubi et verborum ordo ministerium est, non verbum e verbo sed sensum exprimere de sensu.' The final words in this celebrated passage have been adopted as the motto of the ITI.

For anyone interested in translation theory during these years probably the best book on the subject is Hans J. Störig (ed.), *Das Problem des Übersetzens*, published by Wiss, Darmstadt, 1973. Of course, for 2,000 years what most people meant by translation was the translation of great works of literature, or of the Bible, and one of the major books of translation literature of recent years, George Steiner, *After Babel, aspects of language and translation* (Oxford University Press), deals almost exclusively with literature. What he shows, for example, is that you take a speech from Shakespeare's *Cymbeline*, and find that every word is loaded with connotation, and that translation not only has to be a multicultural activity, but one that is multi-faceted.

A seminal work in translation studies, or translatology, or *Übersetzungswissenschaft*, or *traductologie*, was a book published in Canada in 1958, called *Stylistique comparée du français et de l'anglais*, apparently prompted by noticing during a car journey road signs in the two languages which, so far from being *calques* or direct translations, showed the different underlying attitudes or cultures.

Since the 1950s theorists of translation have been trying to come to grips with the sheer complexity of translation, and there has been a veritable deluge of works on translation theory, on formal equivalence, on equivalent effect, on *parole* versus *langue*, on *Botschaftübersetzung*, on hermeneutics, on normative approaches, on categories and cognitive models, on prototype semantics, on the *Gestalt* approach, and many others; there are schools, the *Übersetzungswissenschaft* school, the *Vertaalwetenschap* school, the Leipzig school, the Finnish school. It would all take another half hour even to summarise, so perhaps we had better leave the mountain of translation theory for another time and another paper.

*Since the paper was given *Traduire* has been revamped and now looks quite attractive (author's note).

Session 7: Report of discussion

Rapporteur: Margareta Synning, SwedBank, Stockholm

Following Geoffrey Kingscott's exposé of translation literature the floor was opened to questions and comments.

Karin Band, freelance translator, wanted to add to the list and 'plug somebody German' – Martin Luther, whose writings contain some of the most important translation principles. Nélida Depiante, freelance translator, agreed with the earlier statements on the general invisibility of translators and interpreters in literature but said that interpreters did appear in some war films. Peter Elphick, Foreign Language Services Ltd, remembered reading that the translator had apologised for not having made a good translation of the pact between the Incas and the Spanish invaders – a task which amounted to 60,000 words in four days. He went on to say that he was disturbed by our letting computer engineers work out how to make translations in order to put us out of business. Why are we being asked to tell them? Should we keep our knowledge to ourselves? Albin Tybulewicz, freelance, then rose to point out that Geoffrey Kingscott's coverage had missed out at least half of Europe – Eastern Europe, perhaps partly because of the preoccupation with 1992. He expressed the hope that the conference committee would begin to fill this gap by inviting speakers from Eastern Europe to future conferences and give ITI members the opportunity to meet colleagues from the other half of Europe. Lanna Castellano, freelance, wanted to mention that there is a work by Graham Greene, the title of which she had forgotten, in which one of the characters is a translator. She went on to say that she resents the fact that the ATA has melodrama in its committee rooms – 'we at ITI must put our minds to it!'

Malcolm Greenwood, freelance, wanted to mention the existence of two books: an Albanian novel, '*Le grand hiver*' by Ismail Kadave, published in France. One of its main characters is an interpreter from the time when Albania fell out with the Soviet Union. In the course of his work he learns things which he must keep to himself. The second book was '*The translator's art*' published by Penguin. It is a selection of papers by people who have translated books for 'Penguin classics'. Geoffrey Kingscott, hearing of the omissions, said in his defence that in making his survey he had had to rely on his own memory and that he welcomed additional information. Ben Teague, freelance from Georgia, USA, mentioned a Robert Redford film, *Three Days of the Condor*, and a science fiction novel, *Babel 17*, by Samuel Delany in which the translating profession enters into the plot.

The chairman then invited representatives of professional associations in other countries to outline the activities of their respective organisations.

After presenting AIIC, Jennifer Mackintosh was asked by Robin Inches, freelance, if AIIC maintains any check on the standard of performance of its members. The answer was that no formal check is kept, but that it had been proposed last year to de-classify members' languages. The normal procedure now is to approach members about whom complaints have been received.

The next question, put by Florence Mitchell, freelance, concerned the *Gestalt* approach in relation to interpreting. Jennifer replied that the idea comes from Danica Seleskovitch, Professor and Director of the Sorbonne postgraduate school for interpreters and translators. It can be described very briefly as the attitude that translators deal with texts and contexts, not only with languages. Fernanda Mello, Milan, described the activities of the Italian Association of Interpreters and Translators, after which Betty Howell outlined the translation scene in Canada. Cate Avery, Eiger Translations Ltd, asked Betty Howell what percentage of translators in Canada are not translating into French. The Société des Traducteurs du Québec has 1,700 members, 900 of whom are certified translators. The STQ only keeps track of the language combinations of the certified members, of whom 80 per cent work from English into French, 15 per cent from French into English. In the rest of Canada there is greater demand than in Quebec for other languages, e.g. German and Asian languages.

The next presentation was by Dr M. Schubert, who gave a picture of the translation scene in the German Democratic Republic; he was followed by Eva Eie, who told the audience about translation activities in Norway. After David Lord's presentation of the Société française des Traducteurs, John Graham, Mannesmann Demag AG, said that he often sees advertisements in the French press for multilingual secretaries who 'must also be able to translate'. He asked whether the SFT aims to do anything about this. David replied that no specific action is planned but that SFT is generally trying to educate the public by publicising their activities and campaigns. Robin Inches, freelance, then asked if anybody could tell him how to get mention of activities, networks, etc. in the press. To this Susana Greiss, ATA, New York chapter, replied that the NYCT has a Public Relations committee which releases and sends to the press news about special events and seeks contacts in the media. When ATA held its annual conference in New York a few years ago it was covered in the *New York Times*. Jane Taylor, University of Manchester, commented that it would be welcomed if somebody in ITI wanted to deal with the matter of the press. As a member of the Education and Training Committee she was much impressed by the fact that all the organisations presented seemed anxious to further the education of translators and interpreters. She said that the Education and Training Committee is trying to address the problem of continuing education for the translator. As well as a new ambitious training programme which is under discussion, the committee would like to centralise information on short courses for translators. Jane appealed to the members of regional groups and networks to pass on information on useful sources of continuing education in their own regions. Asked if she meant courses specifically directed at translators Jane said that she welcomed information on any courses that generally may be useful such as introductions to law, book-keeping, etc.

Pamela Mayorcas, freelance, wanted to encourage all efforts to promote the profession. She said that our clients are really only interested in the product, and that there is a tremendous accent on language for business. We have a most important message to try to get across to government: trained translators and interpreters are the people to be used for international communication. John Craddock, freelance, wanted to bring attention to the steadily growing interest in and demand for the Japanese language. He asked if an invitation to the next ITI conference could be extended to the Japanese Translators' Association

Conference summary: A new profile for the language profession

Anthony F. Hartley

School of Cognitive and Computing Sciences, University of Sussex

INTRODUCTION

It has been impressed upon me that this summary of our two-day conference should be both brief and controversial. Brevity requires selectivity, and so I hope that individuals will feel in no way slighted if their names are not linked explicitly here to the issues raised in the course of the proceedings. It would, in any case, be tedious and pretentious of me to summarise ideas developed at eloquent length by the invited speakers. Controversy is a more difficult note to pitch, especially when a lack of time could deny others a right of reply. So if I am not to abuse the luxury of having the last word, then please take these remarks concluding this conference as suggestions for items on the agenda of future meetings of the ITI. In some instances I am merely echoing proposals for further initiatives already voiced.

This was a conference that had imposed no single theme. The papers and panel discussions reflect the wide variety of activities undertaken by members of the translating and interpreting professions, and beyond. And it is precisely on the 'beyond' that I would like to hang this summary, by looking first at our place in the larger community of 'communicators' and then questioning if current patterns of education and training for translators fit them for taking their proper place in this community.

THE PROFESSIONAL COMMUNICATOR

Translation and interpreting are special cases of communication, founded on the existence of language barriers. The 'language industry', a concept touched on by Juan Sager, embraces other professional communicators not directly competent for mediation across languages. Translators and interpreters are necessarily dependent on the communications of others for their livelihood; and those others are increasingly reliant on linguists. How can we foster symbiosis rather than the – not always benign – parasitism that seems to characterise our current relationship with other communicators? This question is at the core of many of the legal and ethical issues raised during that same session and, more generally, underlies the matter of 'client education' so often referred to.

The ITI is to be congratulated on inviting speakers representing two of these professions. We heard from Kate Pool, of the Society of Authors, that literary translators are legally entitled to the copyright on their work and the guarantees that affords. In other words, in the eyes of the law they are first class citizens. They are authors in their own right. This was news, good news, to many. Speaking for one of the support industries for communication, John Murphy stated that 'translation is almost dead easy'. That could sound like bad news, underplaying the specialist foundations of language transfer, until we recall that 'translation' was being used in the context of shifting between data formats on floppy disks. More good news, then, but also a reminder – if any were needed – of how easily confusion can arise between collaborators coming from different disciplines. A common language presupposes a community.

Another group of professional communicators – 'the media' – loomed in the background, rather ominously for the most part. There was, on the one hand, an understandably defensive attitude to working with the media when their ethical standards were visibly wanting. On the other hand, Mike Hollow's account of monitoring foreign broadcasts for and, significantly, *within* the BBC pictured a much happier relationship. Yet another group of communicators – and the source of the overwhelming bulk of material for translation – was not represented among the speakers; perhaps technical authors are struggling for professional recognition in just the same way that we are.

It is essential that we and these other categories of communication specialists should exchange our mutual perceptions, however unflattering, and achieve a better awareness of each other's job profiles and constraints. The ITI has a leading role to play and in so doing will enhance its own professionalism as perceived by other workers in the language industry. It will be a step towards giving greater professional cohesion to an emergent community of interests.

The recognition of a shared and complementary set of aptitudes, distributed fluidly between individuals, under the generic heading of communication, also facilitates career moves across traditional confines, as we heard from our colleagues in Quebec. These confines are already less restrictive. Compare the job descriptions of Doug Embleton's 'language co-ordinator', the community interpreter and the BBC monitor; they variously combine a mix of linguistic, entrepreneurial, managerial, journalistic and 'socio-legal' skills.

Of course, not all translators want to 'move out of the backroom' to the extent of radically changing the outlook of their day-to-day activities. But for the many who do and for the majority who want better informed and more informative contact with their clients, we need to rethink education and training patterns. We need to ask whether the selection procedures – or lack of them – and the organisation typifying our educational institutions today actually promote a hermit mentality. Do they encourage would-be translators to be wallflowers? Do they encourage would-be engineers to shy away from face-to-face conversation? Certainly, there is little evidence in universities – in the UK, at least – of 'overlapping circles' and much evidence of the compartmentalisation said to characterise industry.

What would we like to do about it in an ideal world? What can we do about it in reality? Let us look at the translator's skills and challenge some assumptions about when and how these are best acquired.

THE TRANSLATOR'S SKILL SET

We can thank Hugh Keith for distinguishing a number of essential competences for translators. If we were to consider interpreters also, we would add to this list; but the items he mentions are enough to set the ball rolling.

The first, enhanced mother-tongue competence, is needed not only by translators but by all professional communicators. To emphasise the unifying theme of communication *per se*, why not establish departments where future translators can join students of engineering and science, broadly conceived, in producing (simulated) training or corporate videos, user documentation, and other linguistic materials?

Translating competence, as the term suggests, is the skill whose mastery distinguishes translators from other professions. It will be taught, appropriately, in departments of translation. It is reassuring to see it factored out not only by academics but also by linguists managing training budgets in the commercial environment, like Mike Hollow. Further substance must be given to this notion through research that will inform effective teaching and learning strategies. Their success in defining these specific skills and explaining them to others will be the measure of translators' collective ability to project themselves as a profession.

While the acquisition of procedural competence or 'meta-knowledge' – the ability to access and assess specialist information – is a general goal of education, there is a strong case for addressing within the translation department itself those particular applications of procedural competence of prime, if not unique, interest to translators. These are the acquisition of subject competence and competence in other languages.

SOME COMMON ASSUMPTIONS IN TRANSLATOR TRAINING

I would like to develop these last two elements in the (UK) context of a shrinking pool of candidates with school or undergraduate qualifications in languages. My lead question is: why is it accepted to be easier to train a linguist to become a translator that it is to train a subject specialist to do so? After all, both need to acquire translating competence. That leaves us with the presumption that it is easier to acquire sufficient subject competence than it is to acquire sufficient competence in other languages. I believe this attitude, which recalls the pre-technological origins of translating, to be the uncomfortable structural legacy of an unfortunate historical accident. Posing this question raises others.

Why is subject competence sidelined in much translator education? The subject competence of teachers and the perceived interests of students are biased towards the socio-politico-economic at the expense of the scientific and technical, so giving a false impression of and unbalanced preparation for a professional workload. This handicap could be alleviated by involving staff from scientific and technical departments more prominently in translator education. This is another instance of the need to escape the compartmentalisation and lack of common interest that hinder access to sympathetic subject specialists in other departments. It would be beneficial for students to be tutored not only by specialists in translation as such but also by expert (and possibly monolingual) readers of their translated texts.

Why is it a 'natural' learning progression to move from general language to special language? Do biochemists need to be able to order a beer in Russian before being able to read a journal article in that language? Does the popular culture have priority over the culture of the discipline? The success of Sheffield University's intensive reading courses in Japanese for the purpose of information acquisition answers all three questions with a resounding 'no'. The experience related by Ben Teague puts flesh on the theory.

Why is advanced linguistic competence in other languages a prerequisite for entry to graduate translator training? In the light of the previous point, it is now clear that we can dispense with this barrier to the profession, with the proviso that we design adequate linguistic aptitude tests and appropriate language instruction for those coming from a non-linguistic background. The foundational linguistic and computational research has been done.

A CHANGING CLIMATE

If we free ourselves from all these assumptions, we can begin to imagine the architecture of a translation programme accommodating two broad categories of students. In contrast to the 'syntax-driven' linguists with little initial idea of what is meaningful in a given field, the 'semantics-driven' specialists would have the task of refining their syntactic knowledge in order to select from within an already known space of possible meanings.

The climate is changing rapidly in Europe since the inception of the ERASMUS programme and other educational schemes which credit students for courses followed at participating institutions in other countries. Many, but not all, of these have an integrated language component. They are exerting a pressure for special-purpose language tuition to which the UK has been slow to respond. The structure of higher education in the UK could change dramatically in the next decade. If British institutions do not meet this challenge, the result will be a lop-sided take-up of the exchange opportunities. If they do, they will at the same time be progressing towards refreshing the pool of potential translators.

THE GROWING ROLE OF THE ITI

Graduates in mathematics or software engineering who have studied in three European countries are spoilt for choice. They will not be tempted into translator training at some stage in their career unless the status and rewards of the profession are at least on a par with those of the other areas they could choose. Such recognition can only be promoted by professional bodies like the ITI.

The ITI will undoubtedly extend its role in representing and defending the interests of the profession, in keeping with the energies and activities of its members. It should now have the self-confidence to venture into the important sphere of educating the client. There are many possible facets to this education, but allow me to pick out just one concrete example from this conference – that of telecommuting. Telecommuting (a.k.a. distance working, home working, remote working – a terminologist's headache) is not a pattern of the future in translating; it is the present. What is novel in the ICL experience is the measure of job security enjoyed by the employees. What is important in the ICL experience for us as translators is precisely the fact that it is a proven success from outside the language field. Telecommuting makes demonstrable economic sense even in the hard-nosed world of computer consultancy. This is a model which the ITI could be bringing to the attention of medium- and even large-sized firms who would like to employ staff translators but who are unable to bear the overheads consequential on bringing their translating in-house.

With its current membership at about 1,000, the ITI is near the critical mass for making its influence felt; with more members its voice will be heard even louder. We have already been told that it is good for our education to 'top up and keep up'. It will be good for ITI and the profession if you can persuade other translator and interpreter colleagues to 'sign up and speak up'.

Biographical notes

Karin R.M. Band
Born 1937. Trained at Vienna University Interpreters' School (Akademischer Übersetzer, Diplom-Dolmetscher). Freelance translator and conference interpreter since 1959, with increasing specialisation in medical work. Moved to London in 1963. Publications: *Glossary of the theatre* (Elsevier, 1969); reviews of medical dictionaries in the *British Medical Journal*. Teaching activities: 1959–1962: Junior Lecturer, Vienna University Interpreters' School; 1986: Medical Module, English Update Course, Polytechnic of Central London. Since 1987: organiser and teacher of Medical English for Translators and Interpreters (annual 2-week course). Member of AIIC.

Peter Barber
Fellow of the ITI and also of the Institute of Linguists. He has been a Member of Council since inauguration and is currently serving on the Admissions Committee and as Arbitration Committee convenor. Within the ITI, he is perhaps best known for his work on the Code of Conduct and Standard Terms of Business. He is Managing Director of Able Translations (a well-known and respected corporate member of the ITI) and Chairman of the European Translation Consortium (ETC), a multinational partnership of translation companies formed with the unified Single Market in mind.

Lucy Collard
Born and educated (mostly) in the United Kingdom. Qualifications and work experience: 1974–76: Press and Information Office of Greek Embassy, London; 1976–80: BA (Hons, First Class) in Arabic and French, PCL; 1980–81: MA Area Studies (North Africa and Middle East), SOAS, London University; 1981–86: Appointed Lecturer II, Arabic Section, PCL; 1982: RSA Cert. TEFL (Preparatory); 1986–present: Senior Lecturer, Arabic Section, PCL; 1986–88: Postgraduate Diploma in Linguistics (Distinction). She has travelled and/or lived in Algeria, Egypt, Libya, Morocco, Pakistan, Uruguay, Greece and France.

Rita Day
Born in Switzerland and came to the United Kingdom in 1962 after obtaining a Diploma in Italian, French and German from the School of Interpreting at Geneva University. She has since worked on the freelance market, concentrating on conference interpreting. Her assignments include government departments (Ministry of Defence and Foreign Office in particular) and industry, where she has worked in subjects as varied as data-processing, construction, electronics and chemical subjects, as well as finance and stock exchange. She has experience at all levels, from the technical meetings of engineers to top level ministerial encounters.

Melanie Dean
Studied Modern Languages at Salford University and was awarded a BA(Hons) in French and German in 1984. After graduation, she worked for one year as a management trainee for one of the major clearing banks. Melanie is now a staff translator with Rhône-Poulenc Ltd, in Dagenham, Essex. She is an Associate Member of the ITI and Secretary of the Aslib Technical Translation Group.

Doug Embleton
Senior Linguist of ICI Chemicals & Polymers Ltd, based at Wilton, Cleveland; main languages: French, German, Spanish and Russian. Has wide experience of translating, interpreting, foreign language publicity/advertising and language training. His work on language services in industry has been reviewed by the press, radio and television. Actively involved with several industry/education initiatives and is co-author of a recent publication *Working with German*.

Roger Fletcher
Roger Fletcher is a full-time freelance whose working time is divided between translation of technical and commercial documents from Chinese in the comfort of a modern electronic office, and interpreting in Cantonese in such venues as police stations, prisons and courts. The amount of time spent on each is more a function of market forces than of personal preference.

Michael Francis
Left the BBC in 1961 to join NATO; is now Senior Interpreter, working at all levels, including Ministerial and Summit Conferences. Teaches at the Universities of Brussels and Mons and directed an intensive course in Conference Interpretation at St Catharine's College Cambridge in August 1989.

John Douglas Graham
Born in Scotland in 1939. BA in French, Russian and German, London University. Founder member of ITI. FIL for 20 years after taking the Fellow General examination in German in 1967. Active member of the German BDÜ. Secretary/Treasurer of the International Association for Language and Business. Now involved in the German Terminology Society (Deutscher Terminologie-Tag). With technical and commercial qualifications (materials management and accountancy) in addition to languages, has been Head of Central Translation Services at Mannesmann Demag in Duisburg, Germany since 1980. Has also been lecturing part-time in translation for non-translators at the University of Duisburg for the last four years.

Sue Halbert
Manager of the Consultancy Group within ICL's 300-strong home working operation, CPS Professional Services. A graduate in Mathematics from Exeter University, she joined ICL, the UK computer manufacturer, as a trainee in 1969. Spent early years in systems and technical support within the sales operation, rising to Regional Support Manager in 1977. In 1979 was appointed General Manager of CPS, working from home; post held for three years until returning to full-time on-site working as a Marketing Manager. After a three year career break, returned to ICL in 1987 as a management consultant specialising in the control of remote, home-based networks of staff now popularly called 'teleworking'. Has since extended her knowledge to include all forms of 'flexible working' including job-sharing, part-time working and flexible working hours.

Tony Hartley
Currently engaged on an Alvey project in robust natural language processing; also works as conference interpreter in French. Teaches French CI at University of Surrey;

formerly taught at Bradford where he introduced post-graduates to MT, a field in which he is a consultant. He has just been commissioned to translate a novel shortlisted for the 1988 Prix du Premier Roman.

Mike Hollow
Studied Russian and French at Cambridge. Has worked for BBC Monitoring for 14 years, including several years as a translator of Russian. For the last two years, has been Organiser, Soviet Monitoring: line manager for about 50 linguists engaged in monitoring Soviet broadcasts, with responsibility for recruitment, training and quality control.

Betty Howell
Born in Boston, Massachusetts, has a BA in medieval studies from Barnard College (Columbia University), studied at the University of Munich and received an M Trad from the Université de Montreal. A Montreal resident since 1969, she does freelance translation of French and German to English, is active in the Société des Traducteurs du Quebec, a member of the American Translators' Association, and teaches translation at McGill and Concordia universities.

Hugh Keith
After studying French and German at Oxford and working at a German university, trained as a teacher at York University. Now works as a lecturer on the BA (Interpreting and Translating) course at Heriot-Watt University, Edinburgh and is a founder member of Integrated Language Services, the university's translation and interpreting service to industry and commerce. Works as a freelance translator and interpreter for both British and German clients and as external examiner for a number of universities and polytechnics. Member of the ITI education and training committee.

Geoffrey Kingscott
A translator since 1964; chairman ITI inaugural meetings 1987, chairman first ITI conference 1987, currently chairman of ITI East Midlands regional group; has twice acted as chairman of the annual Translating and the Computer conferences; editor and publisher *Language Monthly* 1983–88, general editor *Language International* since January 1989; language adviser to the first London Language Show to be held in June 1989; member since 1986 *Vorstand of Internationale Vereinigung Sprache und Industrie*, and is organising its 1989 conference.

David Lord
Graduated from ESIT in Paris in 1981. After working for three years as an in-house translator for a French company, went freelance. Has been a SFT committee member for five years and a technical translation tutor at ESIT since 1983.

Martin Lovell-Pank
Born in Argentina and went to Argentine and UK schools. He worked in Argentine and UK banks as a staff translator, then left to study business translation and technical and specialised translation at the Polytechnic of Central London. He is now a freelance translator and interpreter and part-time lecturer in Spanish at the Polytechnic of Central London.

Jennifer Mackintosh
Has been a conference interpreter since 1964. Works for the UN family of organisations, the EC, governments and the private sector. A former AIIC Council member and Vice-President, she is currently convenor of the AIIC Research Committee, and acting convenor of the AIIC Training Committee. From 1980–86, was course leader for the Polytechnic of Central London's course in the techniques of conference interpreting. Since then, as well as her regular interpreting work, has been designing and running intensive language enhancement courses for practising conference interpreters.

Pamela Mayorcas
Took the Polytechnic of Central London's Diploma in Modern Languages and European Studies 1965–68. Her first job was with the Iron and Steel Institute. In 1970 she joined the Foreign Office team which translated the authentic English texts prior to UK accession to the EC. Since 1973, she has worked for the EC Commission, starting as a technical translator; but currently concerned with information and documentation systems for translators. Was awarded an MSc in Information Science by the City University in 1981. Is specially interested in information problems as they apply to translators, including the use of informatin technology, and has published a number of articles on the subject. Has been actively involved with the ITI since its inception.

Fernando Mello
Born in Milan, Italy. Studied languages in England, France and Italy. Trained as a teacher in London. Her first job was with ICI, but since 1975 she has worked for English and Italian companies as a freelance interpreter/translator. Over the last decade she has designed and run a number of courses for young translators. AITI member since 1978, and former AITI council member, she is specially interested in medical translations and eager to write children's books.

Stanley Minett
Founder member of the ITI. He has enjoyed careers in both the Royal Navy (where he learnt Russian) and the construction industry. Having been a part-time freelance translator of Russian since 1960, he became a full-time freelance at the start of 1984 and gets great pleasure from both the work and the friendly contacts he has made through ITI.

John Murphy
Has worked in the computer industry for about 20 years, 10 of them with IBM, and three with his present firm InterMedia Graphic Systems Ltd. He has covered all sorts of commercial applications with both minis and mainframes, but at InterMedia has dealt mostly with text systems.

Christopher Percival
Graduated in languages and law 1960, qualified as a chartered accountant 1963. Worked in Germany and other European countries with an international firm of accountants. Began translating seriously in 1976. Now a full-time freelance translator in accountancy. Published *Glossary of European accounting charts* in 1982. Founding member of the ITI and first Chairman of the ITI North East regional group.

Kate Pool
Educated at Benenden and Exeter, where she read English. Joined the Society of Authors in 1979 and is now Assistant General Secretary, with particular responsibility for members' contracts. She is also Manager of the Society's journal *The Author*, and Secretary of the Translators' Association.

Beryl Rice
Graduated in German with Russian and taught in the United Kingdom, Uganda and Germany before joining ICI in London, first as a translator and then as Head of the Group HQ Languages Unit. Chairman of the Aslib Technical Translation Group 1979–82. Winner of the first Frank Wallwork Memorial Award for services to translation in Demember 1988, which also marked the start of her new career as a freelance translator and consultant where, among other things, she acts as an external examiner for the Polytechnic of Central London and as a Principal Examiner for the Institute of Linguists.

Juan Sager
Studied in Argentina, USA, Scotland and Federal Republic of Germany. Professor of Modern Languages and Head of Department of Language and Linguistics and Centre for Computational Linguistics (CCL) at the University of Manchester Institute of Science and Technology. Chairman of the EC Commission's Advisory Committee of Experts on Transfer of Information between Languages (CETIL).

Julie Slade
Joined Digital Equipment in 1987 as a Translation Manager. Studied at London University and the Polytechnic of Central London. Joined a patent agent as a translator before moving to British Telecom for four years.

Margareta Synning
MA in English and French, Uppsala University. A translator since 1968, is now part-time staff translator with SwedBank, Stockholm, and part-time freelance. Has worked as a court interpreter for many years. Joined the ITI as a founder member in 1986.

Jane Taylor
A graduate of Oxford University, now teaches French at the University of Manchester with a particular interest in translation theory and practice. Has run a module on this area for some years, where professional translators in the widest possible range of specialities, from comic strip to drama, from libretto to novel, from technical to cartoon, have offered workshops to students. Also works as an occasional freelance translator from French, specialising in outdoor pursuits. Has been a member of the ITI since its inception; is a member of its National Council and chairs its Education and Training Sub-Committee.

Ben Teague
Works as a freelance translator in Athens, Georgia. Holds a BA in physics (Rice University); specialises in literature relating to energy, materials, and earth sciences. Has served as secretary, president-elect and president of the American Translators' Association. Translates principally from Russian and German for clients in government and industry.

Hilde Watson
Has wide-ranging experience in the field of languages. Spent most of her career as a translator and conference interpreter. Has also taught conference interpreting in a part-time capacity at Bath University and the Polytechnic of Central London. Freelance work covers international organisations, government departments, industry and the European Communities.

Heather Wheeller
Studied French and German at the Institut Français in London learning Spanish on the way. Did various jobs with languages and some freelance translation. Obtained employment as translator with South American/international bank. Has progressed with the bank in its various forms and with international markets and now heads the Translation Section of Lloyds Bank. Has a keen interest in the ITI and is a member of the Aslib Technical Translation Group committee.

Attendance list

Abdou, Kamar, American University, Cairo, Egypt
Abt, Diana, freelance, Richmond, Surrey
Al-Hamdi, Ahmed, freelance, London
Alexander, Jeanette, freelance, London
Anderson, Janet, freelance, Orpington, Kent
Andreasen, Marie-Josée, UCB, Brussels, Belgium
Ansah, Sara, freelance, London
Arbia, Nicoletta, freelance, London
Arthern, Peter, CEC, Brussels, Belgium
Avery, Cate, Eiger Translations Ltd, Manchester
Awad, Mansour, freelance, Thignonville, France
Bailey, Joy, First Edition, Cambridge
Band, Karin, freelance
Barber, Peter, Able Translations, Baldock, Herts
Barefoot, Brian, freelance, Bradford-on-Avon
Barnes, Sono, Japan Communication Service, Wellington, NZ
Beattie, David, Hoechst UK Ltd, Hounslow, Middlesex
Beck, Gerald, freelance, London
Berger, Bruno, freelance, Hanover, West Germany
Berson, Alan, freelance, London
Betcke, Paul, Finnish Translators Association, Turku, Finland
Bevington, Liz, Laporte Industries, Luton
Birch, Sally, freelance, Teddington, Middx
Bird-Louis, Magda, freelance, Congleton, Cheshire
Bodnar, Clara, Encyclopaedia Britannica, London
Bokx, Hans, Unilever, Vlaardingen, Netherlands
Bonafe, Hugo, student, Manchester
Boothroyd, Paul, freelance, Stuttgart, West Germany
Bothof, Gerrit, Vertaalbureau Bothof, Nijmegen, Holland
Bowen, Monica, Öhrlings Revisionsbyra, Stockholm, Sweden
Bowles, Judy, student, London
Bradhering, Hanna, Translingua, Bonn, West Germany
Braley, Alan, freelance, Knebworth, Herts
Bramall, Gery, freelance, London
Brigham, Fernande, freelance, Kimbolton, Cambs
Brooke, Mary, Pentacom Computers, Newbury, Berks
Brookes, Julie, freelance, Manchester
Brown, Susan, student, London
Brusick, Huguette, freelance, Paris, France
Bruzzone, Marco, Multi Lingua, London
Budiardjo, Suwondo, freelance, London
Buxbom, Kirsty, Rank Xerox, St Albans, Herts
Cairns, John, CBTIP, Ghent, Belgium
Campion, Malcolm, BTI Bureau Services, London
Candeland, Richard, University of Bradford

Cannell, Dinah, freelance, London
Cardoso, Helena, freelance, Bournemouth
Carrington-Windo, Tristam, freelance translator, London
Cassidy, Yvonne, Ickenham, Middx
Castellano, Lanna, freelance, London
Chadwick, Nicolas, freelance, London
Charles, Mary, freelance, London
Charrondière, Annie, freelance, London
Clark, Gunnel, Clark Translations, Wotton-under-Edge, Glos
Clark, Robert, Clark Translations, Wotton-under-Edge, Glos
Clayton, Julie, student, London
Clemensha, Josephine, AMRO Bank, Amsterdam, Netherlands
Coffey, Margaret, freelance, Mönchengladbach, West Germany
Coles, Sue, AA, Basingstoke, Hants
Collard, Lucy, Polytechnic of Central London
Connerton, Lynda, DTI, London
Conrad, Jack, freelance, London
Cooper, Stephen, Grant & Cutler, London
Cordier, Valérie, student, London
Couchman, Charlotte, freelance, London
Cousins, Travers, Sally Walker Language Services, Bristol
Craddock, John, freelance, Maidenhead, Berkshire
Cragie, Stella, freelance, Naples, Italy
Craven-Bartle, Joseph, Spantext, Karlskoga, Sweden
Cronin, Desmond, London
Cronin, Francine, freelance, London
Cross, Graham, freelance, Ewloe, Clywd
Da Silva, Telma, freelance, London
Dahl, Emilio, freelance, Södertälje, Sweden
Dale, Lorna, Metropolitan Police, London
Dalgleish, James, freelance, London
Day, Rita, freelance, London
Dean, Melanie, Rhône-Poulenc Ltd, Hornchurch, Essex
Depiante, Nélida, freelance, Farnborough, Hants
Dewsnap, Robert, freelance, Sölvesborg, Sweden
Drummond, George, freelance, Hamburg, West Germany
Drummond, Helga, freelance, Chandler's Ford, Hants
Duerings, Reinholt, Ink International, Amsterdam
Eie, Eva, freelance translator, Eiksmarka, Norway
Elgingihy, Azza, freelance, Leamington Spa
Elphick, Peter, Foreign Language Services Ltd, Stafford
Embleton, Doug, ICI
Falla, Paul, freelance, Bromley, Kent
Farkas, Hilary, freelance, Bishops Stortford, Herts
Fawcett, Lou, student, Edinburgh
Feather, Peter, Glaxo Group Research, Guildford, Surrey
Fletcher, Roger, freelance
Fleurent, Claude, Rhône-Poulenc Ltd, Brentwood, Essex
Fogarty, Eyvor, freelance translator, London
Forsyth, Mr, DTI, London
Fortune, Maud, Ciba-Giegy, Horsham, West Sussex

Francis, Michael, NATO HQ, Brussels, Belgium
Fraser, Janet, Polytechnic of Central London
Fulton, Michael, 20th Century Translators, Reading
Gallo, Laura, freelance, Slough, Berks
Garner, Michael, freelance, Helsinki, Finland
Gemming, Anna-Lena, Tolk-och översättarinstitutet, Stockholm
Gibson, Carl, student, Guildford, Surrey
Gibson, Paul, ICI, London
Goddard, Richard, freelance, Romford, Essex
Goodwin, Elena, International Sugar Organisation, London
Gosling, Uta, BSI, Milton Keynes, Herts
Graham, John, Mannesmann Demag, Duisburg, West Germany
Greenwood, Malcolm, freelance, Rochdale, Lancs
Greiss, Susana, freelance, New York
Griffin, John, freelance, Battle, East Sussex
Griffiths, Verley, freelance, Rome, Italy
Grisi, Anna, freelance, Venice, Italy
Guard, Nicky, Fokus Bank, London
Guedes, Josette, freelance, London
Hagemann, Wolfgang, Deutsches Institut für Normung, Berlin, FRG
Halbert, Sue, ICL
Hammond, Philippa, freelance, Inverness
Hargreaves, Gillian, freelance, Ruislip, Middx
Harris, David, freelance, London
Harris, Robin, student, London
Hartley, Tony, University of Sussex
Harvey, Jillian, student, Edinburgh
Haydock, Juliet, freelance, Twickenham, Middlesex
Hayward, Judith, freelance, Brighton, East Sussex
Hayward, Oliver, FCO, London
Herbulot, Florence, freelance, Paris, France
Herget, Judy, Engineering Languages, London
Hesselmann, Hubert, freelance Fareham, Hants
Heuss, Wolfgang, SDI, Munich, West Germany
High, Graeme, freelance, London
Hill, Peter, freelance, Dartmouth, Devon
Hinchliffe, Inga-Beth, freelance, Killeberg, Sweden
Hind, Margaret, freelance, London
Hollis, Robin, Interlingua TTI, London
Hollow, Michael, BBC Monitoring Service
Hooper, Raymond, Boehringer Mannheim, Mannheim, West Germany
Horton, Maria, freelance, Aylesbury
Howell, Betty, freelance, Montreal, Canada
Hulme, Anne, freelance, Drayton, Shropshire
Hutchison, Norman, freelance, London
Hutson, John, freelance, East Molesey, Surrey
Inches, Robin, freelance, Sherborne, Dorset
Ingleton, Roy, Legal & Technical Translations, Kent
James, Meriel, Rolls-Royce, Bristol
Jenkins, Susan, ICI, London
Johns, Michael, Volvo Language Service, Gothenburg, Sweden

Jones, Rosemarie, CCAE, Cambridge
Jutet, Monique, freelance, Asnières, France
Kaye, Tony, freelance, Marlingford, Norwich
Keith, Hugh, Heriot-Watt University, Edinburgh
Kelly, Maryse, freelance, Uxbridge, Middx
Kemppainen, Sempo, Interverbum AB, Stockholm, Sweden
Kerr, Marie-Hélène, Inmarsat, London
Kingscott, Geoff, Praetorius Ltd, Nottingham
Kirby, Jean, freelance, Crawley, West Sussex
Klein, Sean, freelance, Willingham, Cambs
Knighton, Paul, freelance, Willingham, Cambs
Knowles, Gary, Link-Line Business Services, Hull
Laffey, Maria, Merz & McLellan, Tyne and Wear
Lanner, Josef, freelance, Abtenau, Austria
Laughlin, Barbara, freelance, Cambridge
Lawson, Pam, freelance, London
Lee, Gillian, Institute of Metals, London
Lemhagen, Gunnar, Tolk-och översättarinstitutet, Stockholm
Lord, David, freelance, SFT
Lovell-Pank, Martin, freelance, London
Lund-Alderin, Christine, Lingua Nordica, Helsinki, Finland
Lynch, Frances, BTI Translation Bureau, London
MacDonald, Aileen, DTI, London
Mackintosh, Jennifer, freelance, AIIC
Maddra, Loekie, Link-Line Business Services, Hull
Maier, Edith, Lexitech, London
Manganaras, Ioannis, freelance, Athens, Greece
Marchinton, Martina, freelance, Ickenham, Middlesex
Marguet, Cathérine, Marguet & Ball, London
Marshall, Sue, Bank of England, London
Maslen, Bill, Interlingua Ltd, London
Mayorcas, Pamela, freelance
Mead, Annie, freelance, West Wickham, Kent
Mello, Fernanda, freelance, AITI
Milican, Daniel, ECHO, Luxembourg
Millward, Pamela, FCO, London
Minett, Stanley, freelance, Great Yarmouth, Norfolk
Misure-Charkham, Deborah, freelance, London
Mitchell, Florence, freelance, Richmond, Surrey
Molyneux-Berry, Aziza, freelance, London
Montanelli, Giulia, freelance, London
Mountford, Jane, BSI, London
Muir, Neil, Angloscan, Shrewsbury, Salop
Nathan, Sven, London
Nice, Richard, University of Surrey, Guildford
O'Connor, Sean, freelance, Tonbridge, Kent
Ogg, Mr G., DTI, London
Oittinen, Liisa, Tolk-och översättarinstitutet, Stockholm
Oliver, David, Oliver Translation Services, Leighton Buzzard
Östling, Leif, freelance, Trangsung, Sweden
Östling, Hillevi, freelance, Trangsung, Sweden

Pacella, Giuseppe, BTI Translation Bureau, London
Pampanini, Danila, freelance, Harrow, Middx
Pascoe, Graham, SDI, Munich, West Germany
Paisley, Herbert, freelance, Theydon Bois, Essex
Pattison, Ann, freelance, Sutton, Surrey
Percival, Christopher, Flambard (European) Ltd, Durham City
Perkins, Paul, freelance, Gateshead, Tyne and Wear
Picken, Catriona, freelance, London
Piehler, Ruth, Öhrlings Revisionsbyra, Stockholm, Sweden
Pollard, Margaret, freelance, Teddington, Middx
Polley, Charles, freelance, Thirsk, North Yorks.
Pool, Kate, Translators' Association
Potts, Marilyn, International Language Consultants, Newcastle-upon-Tyne
Price, Penny, freelance, Mitcham, Surrey
Rapi, Nina, freelance, London
Reier, Nina, freelance, Porsgrunn, Norway
Rice, Beryl, freelance
Roberts, David, Philips Research, East Grinstead, West Sussex
Roberts, Julie, freelance, Farnborough, Hants
Roberts, Keith, Siemens plc, Chertsey, Surrey
Rogers, Marion, freelance, Kettering, Northants
Rosebaum, Peter, freelance, Welwyn, Herts
Rosenthal, Nick, Salford Translations Ltd, Manchester
Ross-Bell, Margaret, freelance, London
Rothwell, Arthur, freelance, Solihull, West Midlands
Rupprecht, Ernst, Technical Translation Associates, Solihull, West Midlands
Ryder, Maria, freelance, London
Sager, Juan Carlos, UMIST
Sainsbury, Simon, Braehler ICS (UK) Ltd, Cambridge
Saleh, Thana, freelance, London
Salice, Luca, freelance, London
Scanlan, Fiona, student, London
Schatz, Hannelore, freelance, London
Schofield, Kerstin, freelance, Abingdon
Schubert, Manfred, Institute for Further Training of Translators and Interpreters,
    Leipzig, GDR
Scoggins, Barbara, Clarendon Consultants Ltd, Littlehampton, West Sussex
Sharma, Rannheid, Nortrans, Brentwood, Essex
Shields, Mike, MIRA, Coventry
Shovelin, Mary, freelance, Brussels, Belgium
Slade, Julie, Digital Equipment Co Ltd, Reading, Berks
Smilde, Cornelis, student, Leuven, Belgium
Smith, Marti, freelance, Cobham, Surrey
Smith, Patricia, freelance, London
Soubrier, Michèle, Rhône-Poulenc Agrochimie, Lyon, France
Spalter, Vicky, Spalter Translations, London
Stagg, Zoe, freelance, Esher, Surrey
Stakic, Jelena, freelance, Belgrade, Yugoslavia
Stanton, Paul, freelance, Norwich
Stephens, Anne, Transtext, Yeovil, Somerset
Stewart, Susan, FCO, London

Stoker, Julie, FCO, London
Stowell, John, Boehringer Ingelheim Ltd, Bracknell, Berks
Stuart, Gordon, freelance, Angus, Scotland
Swoboda, Anna, CBA Translations, Bristol
Sykes, John, Oxford University Press, Oxford
Symonds, Robert, freelance, Bromley, Kent
Synning, Margareta, freelance, Lidingo, Sweden
Taylor, Jane, University of Manchester
Teague, Ben, freelance, Atlanta, Ga, USA
Tennenhaus, Shula, Wordbank Ltd, London
Trentham, Giles, Wordbank Ltd, London
Turkistanli, Ahmet, freelance, London
Tybulewicz, Albin, freelance, London
Varcoe, Ann, Global English, Österskär, Sweden
Varcoe, George, Global English, Österskär, Sweden
Walker, Sally, Sally Walker Language Services, Bristol
Watanabe, S., freelance, East Grinstead, West Sussex
Watson, Hilde, freelance
Watts, Niki, freelance, St Ives, Cambs
Weeks, David, freelance, Farnham, Surrey
Weeks, Josephine, student, Winchester, Hants
Wenman, Tina, freelance, Doncaster, South Yorks
Weston, Diana, freelance, London
Wheeler, Patricia, freelance, London
Wheeller, Heather, Lloyds Bank plc, London
Williams, Jelly, freelance, Oxford
Williams, Rob, freelance, London
Wilson, Barbara, FCO, London
Wilson, Peter, freelance, Sevenoaks, Kent
Winston, Lisa, student, London
Woods, Margaret, freelance, Eastleigh, Hants
Young, Sue, Cave Translations Ltd, London